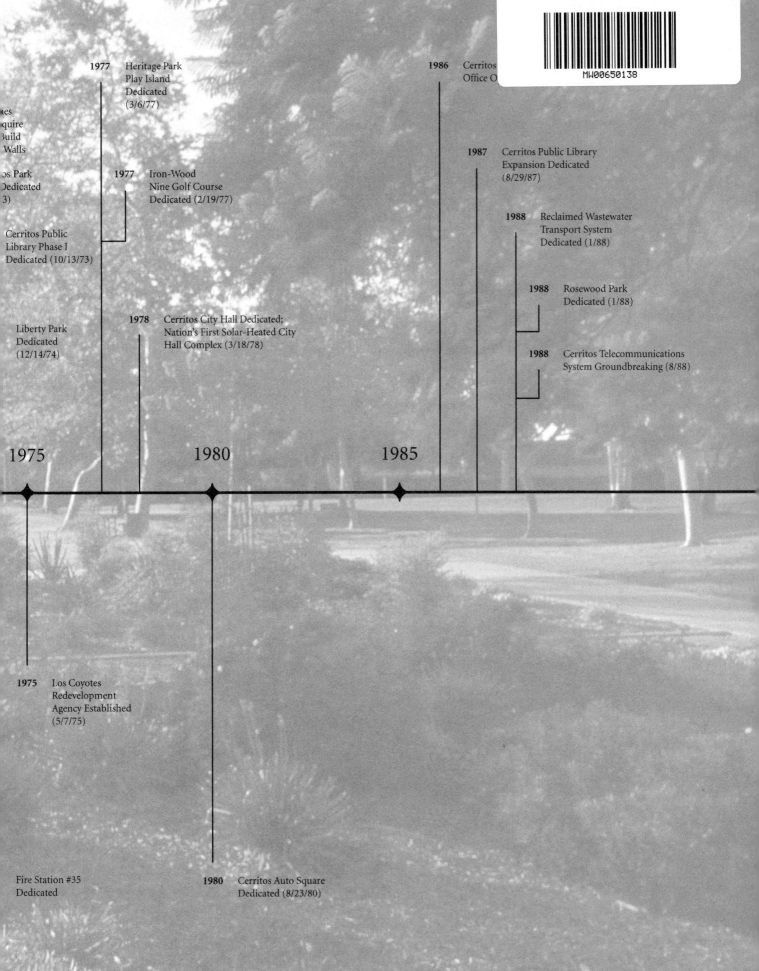

1977 Heritage Park
Play Island
Dedicated
(3/6/77)

1986 Cerritos
Office O

1987 Cerritos Public Library
Expansion Dedicated
(8/29/87)

es
quire
Build
Walls

os Park
Dedicated
3)

1977 Iron-Wood
Nine Golf Course
Dedicated (2/19/77)

1988 Reclaimed Wastewater
Transport System
Dedicated (1/88)

Cerritos Public
Library Phase I
Dedicated (10/13/73)

1988 Rosewood Park
Dedicated (1/88)

Liberty Park
Dedicated
(12/14/74)

1978 Cerritos City Hall Dedicated;
Nation's First Solar-Heated City
Hall Complex (3/18/78)

1988 Cerritos Telecommunications
System Groundbreaking (8/88)

1975 1980 1985

1975 Los Coyotes
Redevelopment
Agency Established
(5/7/75)

Fire Station #35
Dedicated

1980 Cerritos Auto Square
Dedicated (8/23/80)

ÇITY OF ÇERRITOS

CIVIC CENTER · 18125 BLOOMFIELD AVENUE
P.O. BOX 3130 · CERRITOS, CALIFORNIA 90703-3130
PHONE: (562) 860-0311 · FAX: (562) 916-1373
WWW.CI.CERRITOS.CA.US

January 1, 2006

Dear Friend:

We are delighted to express our heartfelt congratulations to the community as we celebrate the City of Cerritos' fiftieth anniversary year. We hope you enjoy this pictorial history book and the story of how the agricultural community of Dairy Valley was established and transformed into the beautiful and thriving City of Cerritos. As we reflect upon the accomplishments of the past fifty years, we believe the next fifty years hold the promise of even greater progress for future generations of Cerritos residents.

Sincerely,

John F. Crawley
MAYOR

Paul W. Bowlen
MAYOR PRO TEM

Gloria A. Kappe
COUNCILMEMBER

Jim Edwards
COUNCILMEMBER

Laura Lee
COUNCILMEMBER

| JOHN F. CRAWLEY | PAUL W. BOWLEN | JIM EDWARDS | GLORIA A. KAPPE | LAURA LEE |
| MAYOR | MAYOR PRO TEM | COUNCILMEMBER | COUNCILMEMBER | COUNCILMEMBER |

Cerritos at 50

Celebrating Our Past and Our Future

City of Cerritos, California

The Donning Company Publishers
184 Business Park Drive, Suite 206
Virginia Beach, VA 23462

Steve Mull, *General Manager*
Barbara Buchanan, *Office Manager*
Pamela Koch, *Editor*
Stephanie Danko, *Graphic Designer*
Amy Thomann, *Imaging Artist*
Debby Dowell, *Project Research Coordinator*
Scott Rule, *Director of Marketing*
Stephanie Linneman, *Marketing Coordinator*

Barbara Bolton, *Project Director*

Library of Congress Cataloging-in-Publication Data

Cerritos at 50 : celebrating our past and our future.
    p. cm.
 "Printed by the City of Cerritos in celebration of its 50th anniversary, this book is based on a manuscript called 'The Story of Cerritos : A History in Progress' by Ms. Marilyn Cenovich ... For this book, Ms. Cenovich's text was edited and expanded by local writer Audrey Eftychiou"--Introd.
 Includes bibliographical references and index.
 ISBN-13: 978-1-57864-349-3 (hardcover : alk. paper)
 ISBN-10: 1-57864-349-X (hardcover : alk. paper)
 1. Cerritos (Calif.)--History. I. Title: Cerritos at fifty. II. Cenovich, Marilyn, d. 2000. III. Eftychiou, Audrey.
F869.C44C47 2006
979.4'93--dc22
                                                                                    2005035808

Printed in the United States of America at Walsworth Publishing Company

Table of Contents

6   Acknowledgements

7   Introduction

1
8   The Natural History of Cerritos

2
14   The Community's Early Origins

3
24   A City Takes Root

4
38   The Founding of Dairy Valley

5
52   A Brand New City: the 1950s

6
64   A Changing City with a New Name: the 1960s

7
76   Forging Ahead through the 1970s

8
96   A Decade of Growth: the 1980s

9
116   Focusing on Service: the 1990s and 2000s

10
148   The City's Enduring Values: Into the Future

170   Appendices

173   Bibliography

175   Index

Acknowledgements

Printed by the City of Cerritos in celebration of its fiftieth anniversary, this book is based on a manuscript called "The Story of Cerritos: A History in Progress" by Ms. Marilyn Cenovich. A librarian at Cerritos Public Library for many years, by all accounts Ms. Cenovich devoted herself completely to documenting our city's fascinating history. While Ms. Cenovich unfortunately passed away in 2000, Cerritos will always be indebted to her for capturing the city's story for future generations. For this book, Ms. Cenovich's text was edited and expanded by local writer Audrey Eftychiou, who also gathered more than 260 photos to illustrate the city's past and present. Ms. Eftychiou also researched and wrote the sidebar information and conducted interviews with several longtime residents.

Many people aided in the publication of this book, most importantly the Cerritos City Council and City Manager Art Gallucci, Recreation Services Superintendent Joe Mendoza, and Cerritos Librarian Padmini Prabhakar. Local photographer Marcus Tate contributed immensely to the city's photo collection.

Several longtime area residents generously provided family memories and photos, including the Barbaria family, Linda Long Bruinsma, Myrtle Franz, C. R. Gutierrez, Manuel and Sigifredo Muñoz, and Annie Troost and her grandson, Jeff Troost. Many thanks also go to the Cerritos Chamber of Commerce and Executive Director Catherine Gaughen; Kristen Habbestad and the Cerritos College Office of Public Affairs; Cerritos resident Michael White Horse Aviles, for his expertise on the Gabrieleno/Tongva Indians; John Heller of the Electric Railway Historical Association of Southern California, who provided historical photos; Steve Iverson, historical curator for the Rancho Los Cerritos Historic Site, who helped verify early chapters for accuracy; and Sue Ann Robinson and Lana Johnson of the Long Beach Museum of Art, for generously providing paintings from the museum's collection.

Sincere gratitude goes to Dr. and Mrs. Edward and Veronica Bloomfield and their daughter, Veronica Elizabeth Bloomfield, who generously shared their one-of-a-kind photographs of early Artesia. These photographs, from the pictorial history *Images of America: Artesia 1875–1975*, were compiled by Mrs. Bloomfield's father, Albert O. Little, who came to Artesia in 1926 and lived to become one of its most illustrious leaders and most passionate supporters. His efforts toward historical preservation have continued with the opening of the Artesia Historical Museum in fall 2005, located at 18644 Alburtis Avenue. Designed with ABC Unified School District students in mind, the museum will help ensure that our region's rich and colorful past is never forgotten.

Finally, this book is dedicated to the past, present, and future residents of our city. Cerritos is a special place because of the dedicated residents who actively contribute to the betterment of the community.

When any baby is born, his or her personality, strengths, dreams, and successes remain a mystery for years to come. But there's always a little twinkle in the eye that offers a clue.

So it was for the City of Cerritos. When our community was first "born" five decades ago, residents had no way to predict its great future, but there was certainly a spark from the very start.

Cerritos was incorporated on April 24, 1956, as the City of Dairy Valley, a pastoral community of dairy farms, cows and chickens, dirt roads, and sugar beet fields. People were few, with more than one hundred thousand cows outnumbering the humans by nearly thirty-to-one.

But the community pride and progressive thinking that have become Cerritos trademarks were evident nonetheless. Within a few short years, citizens acknowledged that rising land values and property taxes had made dairy farming uneconomical. During a special election on March 2, 1965, voters agreed to open up the dairy fields to new homes, laying the foundation for the diverse, thriving, and beautiful community we enjoy today. A name change followed soon after when a city contest produced the name "Cerritos," a nod to the original Spanish land grant that was a prominent part of the region's history.

With gracious new homes under construction citywide, Cerritos soon became the fastest growing community in California, and city leaders saw the need to carefully guide our city's growth. The first Cerritos General Plan, adopted on October 27, 1971, laid out a vision for a park-like community with acres of green open space, beautiful neighborhoods, services and shops close to homes, and a smart mix of commercial and industrial development.

That vision has certainly become reality, and our city's unique personality, strengths, dreams, and successes have come to fruition. Today, Cerritos is a close-knit community of diverse and active residents, world-class facilities, top-notch public services, financial security, and beautiful vistas. We are thrilled not only to celebrate our city's fifty-year milestone, but also our community's tremendous successes. We hope you and your family enjoy this pictorial history, which will lead you through our city's earliest days to its glorious future.

The Natural History of Cerritos

1

Climate

Cerritos is located on a 275-mile-long strip of coastal land that runs from Santa Barbara to San Diego. Bordered on the east and north by mountains, the entire strip enjoys a Mediterranean climate, with warm-to-hot summers, mild winters, and occasional rain.

Within the Los Angeles Basin, Cerritos has a very unique climate called "semi-marine." In this particular zone, the fog that often covers local beaches rarely reaches our city limits, but a cooling breeze nearly always makes its way up the San Gabriel River channel. This phenomenon helps protect Cerritos from the stifling heat and smog neighboring cities bear each summer, as well as the Santa Ana winds that menace the cities closer to the mountains. This nearly perfect environment has remained an attraction—for the region's earliest settlers, later for dairies and farmers, and today for the fifty-two thousand residents who call Cerritos home.

Up on the Divide, *1939, a 24″ by 30″ oil-on-canvas by George Henry Melcher. Collection of the Long Beach Museum of Art, Long Beach, California, #85-6.11. Photograph © 1999 Long Beach Museum of Art.*

Private Road, *1939, a 24″ by 30″ oil-on-canvas by George Henry Melcher. Collection of the Long Beach Museum of Art, Long Beach, California, #96.16. Photograph © 1999 Long Beach Museum of Art.*

First Settlers

Anthropologists agree that Native American Indians were our area's first settlers, arriving as hunters in search of prey. As more and more set up camp with their families, the Native Americans formed into villages of fifty to one hundred people. All totaled, scientists believe that up to seven hundred thousand Native Americans lived in California before European settlers arrived, with the groups speaking twenty-two separate languages and more than two hundred dialects.

The Native Americans who lived in the Cerritos area called themselves Tongva (People of the Earth). Later, the Tongva would be named "Gabrielenos" after the mission that they built, Mission San Gabriel Arcángel.

The Gabrielenos were the largest group of Southern California Indians, with a reputation for being the wealthiest and most highly developed. The area that the Gabrielenos occupied as their home is now Los Angeles and the surrounding areas, from the San Fernando Valley to San Bernardino, along the coast from Huntington Beach to Long Beach, as well as the islands of Catalina and San Nicholas. The men would travel between islands and the mainland in plank

This ca. 1900 photo by Hervey Friend shows an enduring view of the Sierra Madre Mountains, with glimpses of Mount Waterman, Charlton Flats, and Mount Baldy (once known as Mount San Antonio). Courtesy of the University of Southern California, on behalf of the USC Specialized Libraries and Archival Collections.

boats called *ti'at*. Early records show that the Gabrielenos lived in simple reed and willow homes called *ki'ish*, with an opening at the top to let smoke out. Both men and women wore their hair long, and most went bare-skinned or cloaked themselves in rabbit fur or deer skin for warmth.

The Gabrielenos lived off the land, deriving food from the animals or plants that could be gathered, snared, or hunted, and grinding acorns as a staple. They wove intricate baskets and fashioned vital utensils and tools from wood, shells, bone, and soapstone. Local herbs were used for medicine, food, and dye for their baskets. The Gabrielenos also bartered with other local villages, perhaps trading skins and acorns for pottery or other necessities. When their work was done, Gabrieleno families invented many kinds of games, loved to bathe, sang songs, and told stories.

While no Native American village sites have been found within Cerritos city limits, many have been found nearby, including Tibahangna and Puvunga in Long Beach.

Left: Members of today's Gabrieleno Tongva Band of Mission Indians display the traditional regalia of their tribe. Pictured from left to right are Two Moon Woman (Dee Roybal), Guiding Young Cloud (Andy Morales), and Chief Red Blood (Anthony Morales). Photo courtesy of Michael White Horse Aviles.

Below: Two contemporary young ladies, dressed in traditional garb, depict a scene that would have been typical of the early years of the Gabrieleno tribe. Pictured are Little Fawn (left) and Hummingbird (right) representing today's Gabrieleno Tongva Band of Mission Indians. Photo courtesy of Michael White Horse Aviles.

2

The Community's
Early Origins

Early Explorers

The lives of the Gabrielenos and the entire future of the region took a turn beginning in the late 1400s when European explorers set sail to America. Through the sixteenth and seventeenth centuries, a string of swashbucklers made their way to the West Coast hoping to establish colonies, develop money-making industries, and, later, to set up elaborate commercial trade routes to Asia.

The country of Spain was among the first to gain a strong foothold in our region. With his eye on the entire West Coast, in 1765 King Carlos III sent one of his best advisors, José de Gálvez, who first took charge in Mexico, then moved up the uncharted frontiers to the north and west, starting new towns with donated funds and volunteer troops.

The California Missions

Hoping to secure the most desirable areas, Gálvez recruited a Franciscan priest named Father Junípero Serra to develop missions, with the central goal of "civilizing" the Native Americans and converting them to Christianity. A military force led by Captain Gaspar de Portolá guarded the missions and ensured the Native Americans' cooperation.

On July 16, 1769, Mission San Diego de Alcalá was founded as the first of a chain of twenty-one missions to be established along the California coast. As the Serra-Portolá expedition blazed a trail up north, Father Juan Crespí, who accompanied them as chaplain, described in his diary "a very spacious valley, well grown with cottonwoods and sycamores, among which ran a beautiful river from the north-northwest.... It has good land for planting all kinds of grain and such. It has all the requisites for a large settlement." This proved to be one of the earliest descriptions of the Los Angeles Basin.

Establishment of the missions and "conversion" of the Native Americans was slow and grueling. It took years to build shelter and establish enough crops and cattle so that the settlements would be self-sufficient. Supplies came just once a year by ship from Mexico. The colonies were at first a drain on the Spanish economy and thought to be too fragile to survive, but to fend off encroachment by other European countries, Spain ordered the team to proceed. On September 8,

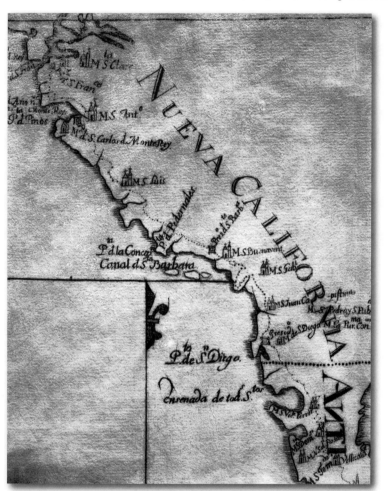

This map of the El Camino Real, upper California, published in 1787, shows the chain of California missions located up and down "Nueva California." Courtesy of the University of Southern California, on behalf of the USC Specialized Libraries and Archival Collections.

Father Serra Celebrates Mass at Monterey, *ca. 1870, an oil-on-canvas by Leon Trousset. Courtesy of the California Historical Society, Fine Arts Collection, FN-31586.*

Franciscan fathers were said to have scattered mustard seeds to mark the trail as they traveled from mission to mission. The tall plants remained for decades, as shown in this ca. 1902 photo. Courtesy of the University of Southern California, on behalf of the USC Specialized Libraries and Archival Collections.

This early painting of Mission San Gabriel was published in Alfred Robinson's book Life in California, *ca. 1838–1846. Courtesy of the University of Southern California, on behalf of the USC Specialized Libraries and Archival Collections.*

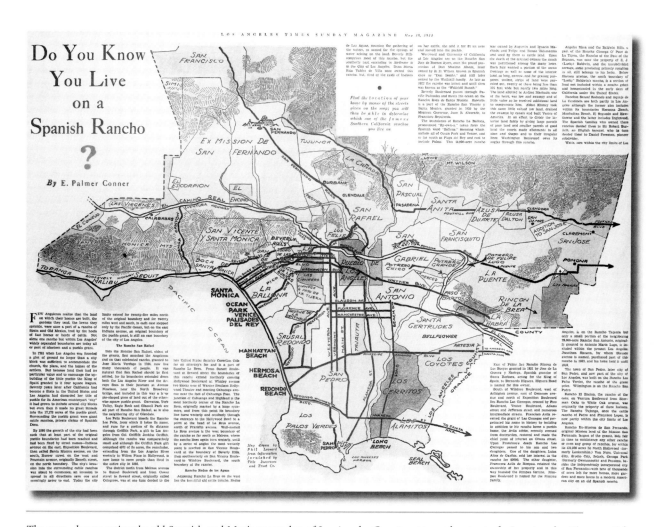

The map, documenting the old Spanish and Mexican ranchos of Los Angeles County, appeared as part of a Los Angeles Times *article by E. Palmer Conner published on May 10, 1931. Courtesy of the University of Southern California, on behalf of the USC Specialized Libraries and Archival Collections.*

1771, Mission San Gabriel Arcángel was established as the fourth mission and the one that would have the most direct influence over our region.

A new town, called el Pueblo de la Reina de los Angeles, was founded soon after in 1781 using craftsmen and experienced farmers from Mexico and, of course, Native American labor. Slowly, the area began to prosper, with herds of cattle and sheep growing by the day and fields, orchards, and vineyards blossoming with the promise of crops. Barley and oats began to replace native grasses, and the entire Los Angeles Basin soon became covered with yellow mustard flowers grown from seeds the settlers had scattered.

Spanish Land Grant

The wilderness that is now Cerritos went first to the hands of a Spanish soldier. Three years after Mission San Gabriel was established, three men from Portolá's first expedition approached the governor and asked permission to graze cattle on land near the mission. Their request was approved, with the stipulation that the land would continue to belong to the king of Spain. With this agreement, Corporal José María Verdugo accepted the very first Spanish land grant of about thirty-five thousand acres on what is now Glendale and Burbank, and he named it Rancho San Rafael. A second grant was bestowed to Juan José Dominguez, who named his seventy-five thousand acres Rancho San Pedro.

José Manuel Pèrez Nieto was granted the third and largest plot. Originally named La Zanja, and later Rancho Los Nietos, the grant covered three hundred thousand acres of what are today the cities of Cerritos, Long Beach, Lakewood, Downey, Norwalk, Santa Fe Springs, and part of Whittier, Huntington Beach, Buena Park, and Garden Grove.

Records show that Nieto was a soldier who had accompanied the 1769 Serra-Portolá expedition as far as the new mission of Velicatá in Baja California. Nieto was stationed at the Monterey presidio in 1773 and at San Diego in 1777. The garrison roster at San Diego lists Nieto as a married soldier, thirty-four years old, illiterate, and Spanish. Nieto settled

into a twenty-foot-square adobe home, along with his wife, two children, and his mother. As his family grew, a small community called Los Nietos grew around the original adobe. When he died in 1804 as the wealthiest man in California, Nieto bestowed the house to his widow and five children, with his eldest son Juan José acting as manager.

Life on the Ranchos

Life on the ranchos was hard, but conditions continued to improve. Soon after California fell under Mexican rule in 1822, full ownership of the ranchos was granted to the individuals who had first claimed them years earlier, including the Nieto family. New Mexican regulations encouraged overseas commerce, and trade soon flourished. The industrious ranchos began churning out much-desired cattle hides, beef tallow, and other products for the rest of the world. The families now lived a comfortable life, hiring specialized servants and using their profits to buy clothing, furniture, food, and tools from across the country. This marked the start of the great "pastoral" period of our region, with the nearby missions and pueblos thriving and the land covered with vineyards, fields, and hundreds of thousands of head of long-horned cattle.

Top: This photo of an old adobe home, what remained of the sprawling Rancho Los Nietos, appeared in the October 1934 issue of Westways. *Vines, bushes, and grass had overtaken the old residence. Courtesy of the University of Southern California, on behalf of the USC Specialized Libraries and Archival Collections.*
Bottom: The Rancho Los Cerritos ranch house, built in 1844 by John Temple, is now owned by the City of Long Beach and serves as a historic museum. The site is located off Long Beach Boulevard near the Virginia Country Club. Courtesy of the University of Southern California, on behalf of the USC Specialized Libraries and Archival Collections.

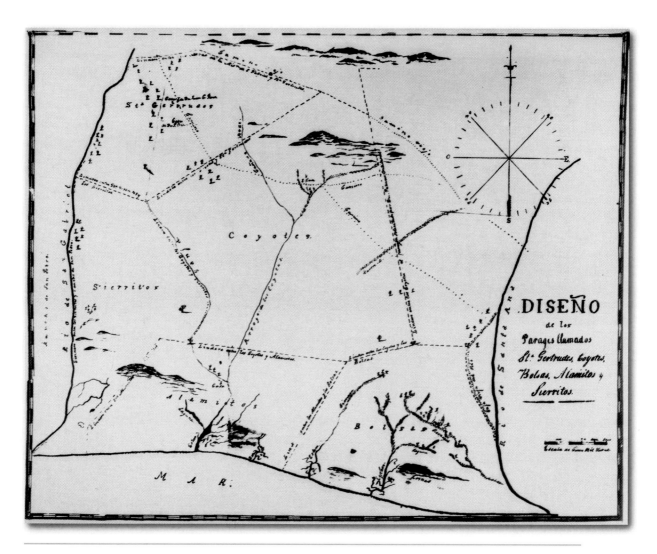

This undated diseño (sketch) of Long Beach shows a wide swath labeled "Coyotes" and an area known as "Sierritos," or little hills. This may have inspired the city name, Cerritos. Courtesy of the University of Southern California, on behalf of the USC Specialized Libraries and Archival Collections.

In New Hands

Amid the arrival of a growing number of foreign settlers and the Mexican government's new efforts to nationalize church property, Juan José Nieto's children became concerned that others might lay claim to their land. In 1834, Nieto's family asked for reconfirmation of ownership from the governor. The governor did confirm the land to Nieto's heirs but divided it into five ranchos.

Over the next ten years, many of Nieto's heirs sold their smaller ranchos to new owners, but Juan José Nieto retained the largest plot. Called Rancho Los Coyotes, the land covered 48,825 acres that included the Coyote Hills, most of Coyote Creek, and much of the land that would one day become Cerritos. Juan José built a gracious hilltop home on his property in 1831, near the location of the Los Coyotes Country Club in Buena Park.

Juan José Nieto sold his plot to Juan Bautiste Leandry, a Sicilian-Italian shop owner from Los Angeles, who renamed the site Rancho La Buena Esperanza ("The Good Hope"). While Leandry died two years later, his wife, Francesca

Uribe Leandry, remarried and lived there with her new husband, Francisco de Campo, for the next twenty years.

Through the 1830s and 1840s, cattle ranching remained the area's main occupation. Native Americans continued to make up much of the labor force, and days were filled with rodeos, the branding of calves, and the drying of cattle skins for trade. Cowhides were traded to New England merchants, with many shipped to the Boston area for conversion to leather goods. The best tallow was kept for making soap and candles on the ranchos while the rest was shipped to the mines of Mexico and South America for use as candles. Much of the beef was left to rot though the best was dried into beef jerky or given to the Native Americans who worked the ranchos. Nearly everyone rode horses, and local residents became famous for their horsemanship. The ranchos also became renowned for their hospitality, hosting frequent celebrations and providing a comfortable stop for travelers on their way to Los Angeles. The Southern California cattle market boomed a second time from 1848 through the early 1850s when newly rich gold miners from the north were willing to pay top dollar for beef.

Ranch Divisions

While local ranchers hoped this "grand fiesta" would never end, events of the 1850s soon put a damper on the celebration. Cattle ranchers in other states began to move their cows to the prosperous West, arriving with better quality animals. Miners and connoisseurs from San Francisco were no longer willing to pay top price for beef that now seemed stringy and tough. Soon the market for Southern California cattle disappeared, and the ranchers who had become used to the finest things in life were instead mortgaging pieces of their property. Following scattered battles up and down the state, an 1848 treaty ended the

This ca. 1877 oil-on-canvas painting by James Walker (1818–1889), entitled Cattle Drive #1, *depicts a typical scene during our area's rancho period. Gift of Mr. and Mrs. Reginald Walker. Courtesy of the California Historical Society, Fine Arts Collection, FN-16020.*

Music and celebrations were an integral part of California's "pastoral" period. This oil-on-canvas painting by Harry Humphrey Moore (1844–1926) is entitled Woman Playing Guitar *(also* Spanish Girl*). Gift of James J. Coyle. Courtesy of the California Historical Society, Fine Arts Collection, FN-31527.*

Mexican-American War, and California was admitted as an American state on September 9, 1850. At the same time, hundreds of American pioneers who had arrived on the West Coast in search of gold now hoped to settle down on farms. Many moved on to the ranchos and became squatters.

While the Treaty of Guadalupe Hidalgo had assured local citizens of Mexican descent that their property would remain their own, in 1851 a federal land commission required the families to prove their ownership. In most cases, this was difficult. Business on the ranchos had been conducted very casually for decades, and few families held acceptable surveys or paperwork. Witnesses were allowed to testify to the ranchos' boundaries, but it was difficult and expensive for most families to take their lawyers, translators, and witnesses to San Francisco for the hearings. Over five years, more than 800 cases were tried involving more than nineteen million acres. More than 500 claims were approved, 275 were rejected, and the rest were withdrawn.

Because they had stashed away grant documents and a formal land survey, Francesca de Campo and Andres Pico won official ownership of Rancho Los Coyotes in 1855. Mrs. de Campo had inherited the land from her husband, while Pico was said to have loaned money, cattle, or goods in exchange for half ownership.

This bounty had only lasted a few years when, in the late 1850s, Pico and de Campo experienced financial troubles and sold Rancho Los Coyotes to Abel Stearns, a Massachusetts native and seaman who arrived in Los Angeles seeking his fortune in 1829. After hauling cowhides for a few years, Stearns had set up a small store in Los Angeles where he invited local ranchers to trade their cowhides for other products. When trade ships arrived from the Northeast, Stearns would sell the hides for cash or more goods.

Slowly amassing a fortune, Stearns (at age forty-two) married Arcadia Bandini, the beautiful fourteen-year-old daughter of an important San Diego citizen, in 1841. The couple's large adobe home on the plaza in Los Angeles, called "El Palacio," soon became the social center of Southern California. Stearns became one of the richest and most respected citizens in the pueblo, serving in local government and later as a state assemblyman. By 1860, he had acquired all but two of the original Nieto ranchos, including the land that is now Cerritos, with property from San Bernardino to the Mexican border.

As the fortunes of the ranchos rose and fell, so did the fortune of Abel Stearns. Severe floods in 1861 and 1862, including two solid weeks of rain, changed the course of rivers and washed away many of the original adobe homes of the "golden days." The floods were followed by the worst drought ever seen in Southern California. Thousands of cattle died, and hoards of crickets devoured anything left that was green. Smallpox devastated the region, and property values in the "cow counties" plummeted.

Delinquent in taxes, Abel Stearns nearly lost all of his property in 1868 before an old friend named Alfred Robinson convinced a group of San Francisco investors to form a land-sale company called the Robinson Trust, otherwise known as the Los Angeles and San Bernardino Land Company. The syndicate saved Stearns from bankruptcy, giving him $50,000 to settle his debts plus one-eighth of the profits. The team began a marketing campaign to entice buyers from the eastern United States and Europe, as well as soldiers returning from the Civil War. New rail lines and the California Immigration Union encouraged the new settlers. The Robinson Trust sold more than twenty thousand acres in its first year, but Abel Stearns wouldn't live to see his second fortune. He died of a sudden illness in 1871 while on a trip to San Francisco.

Top: *Designed by Major R. S. Garnett of the U.S. Army, the California State Seal was adopted at the Constitutional Convention in 1849 before California became a state. Minor changes were made later, in 1937.*

Bottom: *By 1860, Abel Stearns (pictured ca. 1840–1860) had become the largest landowner in California. Before his death in 1871, he also served as Los Angeles city treasurer and mayor. Courtesy of the University of Southern California, on behalf of the USC Specialized Libraries and Archival Collections.*

3

A City Takes Root

*J*ust a few decades later, no marketing was necessary to draw new settlers to the Los Angeles Basin. With its perfect climate and growing towns, Southern California had become a destination for adventurous families seeking a new life "out West." More than one hundred thousand people lived in the city of Los Angeles in 1900, with several other thousands in outlying communities that were surrounded by farms.

A man named Henry E. Huntington helped this growth by devising a new system of rail lines to connect the growing burgs. He launched construction of his Pacific Electric Railway in 1902, and within just a few years, the very first "Red Cars" were carrying passengers from Los Angeles to the new town of Long Beach. As the rail system grew, farmers realized they could leave their fields and commute to better paying jobs in the cities. With convenient transportation as a draw, the local population boomed. In the span of a decade, the city of Long Beach alone grew from twenty-two hundred people to more than eighteen thousand residents.

At the same time, the town of Artesia was flourishing. The community had been established in 1875 with the opening of the Artesia schoolhouse on the corner of 183rd Street and Alburtis Avenue. The area's free-flowing Artesian wells, which had given the town its name, had created a successful farm region, rich with grapes, sugar beets, other vegetables and fruits, ferns and flowers, and poultry and dairy farms.

By the turn of the twentieth century, smaller towns were eager to gain the prestige, convenience, and economic

By the turn of the twentieth century, Los Angeles was a growing metropolis of one hundred thousand residents, surrounded by working farms. This photo (ca. 1895–1915) looks north from Elysian Park. Courtesy of the University of Southern California, on behalf of the USC Specialized Libraries and Archival Collections.

benefits of becoming a Red Car stop, so in 1906, when the line was extended to Santa Ana, leaders of Artesia worked steadily to convince Pacific Electric to build through their town. A new station was built on Artesia's Main Street (what is today Pioneer Boulevard), with a small green park across the street for waiting passengers. Artesia's business district soon flourished, with shops and offices clustered between today's 186th Street and the Pacific Electric station. An old schoolhouse was sold and moved in 1910 to a new site on Pioneer Boulevard where Postma's Furniture Store is located today. The schoolhouse became a general store with a hotel upstairs, while a new brick Artesia Grammar School was built nearby. The next stop to the east was a new town called Waterville, which was eventually renamed Cypress.

This photo is believed to show the celebration marking the opening day of the Pacific Electric Line in Long Beach. Throngs of visitors crowded the streets and pier, festooned with flags. Courtesy of the University of Southern California, on behalf of the USC Specialized Libraries and Archival Collections.

Thanks in part to the Red Cars, the Los Angeles area continued to grow through the early 1900s, with the city of Los Angeles doubling its population every ten years. Outlying communities such as Artesia also continued to grow, as new local industries continued to demand more and more workers. Many people commuted daily across the basin by railway or car, and Artesia became a successful "bedroom community" of four thousand residents.

Farming Overtakes Ranching

By this time, most of the longhorn cattle that had roamed the area the previous century had made way for crops, and farms sprawled across the land. The well-known Gorinis family farm, along South Street between Bloomfield and Shoemaker Avenues, produced acre upon acre of daffodils, dahlias, and other flowers. Other local farmers raised a variety of corn known as Orange County Prolific, which would grow to fourteen feet tall. The variety produced a few edible ears but was most valuable for the long, thick stalk and leaves that made excellent food for livestock. The Pacific Electric hauled tons of sugar beets, sweet potatoes, and other goods from Artesia to stops throughout the Southland.

The area was also home to several vineyards, and George Frampton Sr. and O. J. Thompson ran a successful winery near the intersection of Pioneer and Artesia Boulevards. Small local dairies cropped up, supplying milk to the Harvey Smith cheese factory in Norwalk and the Lily Condensed Milk Company in Buena Park.

Henry E. Huntington (here ca. 1900) inherited a fortune and chairmanship of the Southern Pacific Railway from his uncle. He later became the region's largest landowner and a collector of rare books and art. Courtesy of the University of Southern California, on behalf of the USC Specialized Libraries and Archival Collections.

The town of Artesia became official with the construction in 1875 of this two-story schoolhouse at the corner of today's 183rd Street and Alburtis Avenue. Forty-four students, from Dairy Valley and Artesia farm families, were enrolled on opening day. Images of America: Artesia 1875–1975.

Artesia's first store, offering general merchandise for local farm families, opened in 1882 on today's Pioneer Boulevard. The store, pictured here in 1895, was later sold to the Frampton family. It housed the local post office. Images of America: Artesia 1875–1975.

Barefoot students from the Artesia Schoolhouse pose on the building's front steps in this turn-of-the-century portrait. The building's entrance had two board planks, one for boys and the other for girls. A wood-burning stove warmed its classrooms. Images of America: Artesia 1875–1975.

Artesia's downtown continued to develop near the turn of the twentieth century with the addition of this two-story hotel and mercantile, built next door to the Frampton Store in 1904. Images of America: Artesia 1875–1975.

The Red Car station was located on the northeast side of the tracks that still pass through Pioneer Boulevard. Passengers waited for their trains at a lush park across the street, complete with a gazebo and drinking fountain surrounded by palm trees. Images of America: Artesia 1875–1975.

The Frampton family was responsible for Artesia's first brick building, constructed in 1905 at the southwest corner of Pioneer Boulevard and 187th Street by the Scott and Frampton Company. The building housed a store and meeting hall. Images of America: Artesia 1875–1975.

The Red Cars Come to Town

As the top brass at Pacific Electric Railway began planning a new line from Los Angeles to Santa Ana in the early 1900s, the route that was first sketched ran through Orange, Fullerton, and Whittier. Fortunately for Dairy Valley, plans were changed.

When the thirty-four-mile route opened for service on November 6, 1905, the Santa Ana Line branched off from the Long Beach Line at Watts, traveling southeast straight to Fourth Street in Santa Ana with stops in Lynwood, Clearwater (Paramount), Bellflower, Artesia, Waterville (Cypress), Stanton, and Garden Grove. Painted a vivid crimson, the trains were dubbed "Red Cars." Residents rejoiced, and business boomed in downtown Artesia.

According to the Electric Railway Historical Association, the Santa Ana Line was a double-track system that featured "superior equip-

Artesia's thriving downtown soon became a familiar stop on the Pacific Electric line between Los Angeles and Santa Ana, which opened for service in 1905. With commuters passing through daily, Artesia's business district flourished. Images of America: Artesia 1875–1975.

ment...on par with the best lines." The route was used mainly to transport citrus fruits, crops, and freight to Los Angeles. Nevertheless, with the slogan "Comfort, Speed, Safety," the line also attracted nearly a million passengers each year during its first few decades. With its quick diagonal route, the line boasted better-than-average operating speeds, beating highway travel hands-down—at least until Firestone Boulevard (now the Santa Ana Freeway) was completed in 1935.

While ridership on the Pacific Electric slowly declined with the popularity of automobiles, the train system enjoyed resurgence during World War II as patriotic motorists parked their cars to conserve oil. From 1944 to 1947, more than two million passengers climbed aboard the Santa Ana Line each year. Nevertheless, by 1950, the line was cut back to Bellflower, and Pacific Electric suggested that residents past that point, including those in Artesia and Dairy Valley, find other means of transportation. Dwindling to just 181,167 passengers per year, the very last train was sent down the tracks in May 1958.

For more information on the Pacific Electric Red Cars and the Santa Ana Line, visit the Pacific Electric Railway Monument at Trask and Newhope Avenues in Garden Grove or the Red Car Museum at the corner of Main and Electric Avenues in Seal Beach, (562) 683-1874.

This site plan shows the Artesia Pacific Electric Railway Depot, a short walk from the Hotel Artesia and other downtown establishments. The depot could be reached at telephone number Downey 5548. From the book Pacific Electric Stations, *courtesy of the Electric Railway Historical Association of Southern California.*

Top: *Now a thriving international marketplace, Artesia's Main Street (now Pioneer Boulevard) was once the "metropolis" for miles around. Farm families relied on Main Street for shopping, mail, and the errands of daily life.* Images of America: Artesia 1875–1975.
Bottom: *Commemorating the very first lighting of street lamps along Pioneer Boulevard in 1927, the community celebrated with a parade and a picnic with free hot dogs, soft drinks, and cotton candy. School was closed for the occasion.* Images of America: Artesia 1875–1975.

With the local agricultural market booming, farm irrigation soon depleted the area's natural Artesian wells, which had once been free-flowing. Most farmers now found it necessary to look below ground for the water they needed, and it is said that the sound of water pumps could be heard across the fields every morning. Families that couldn't afford pumps would have their children take turns at hand-pumping until their water tanks were full.

Small-Town Life

Along with tending the fields and walking along dirt roads to school, life in the area was typical of small-town America. Thelma Ryan, who later married the future president and became First Lady Patricia Nixon, spent many years in Artesia and Dairy Valley as one of the many children who enjoyed all the area had to offer. As Julie Nixon Eisenhower wrote in her mother's biography, young Thelma would often accompany her parents on buggy trips to downtown Artesia, which consisted of a bank, a barbershop, two blacksmiths, a hardware store, Scott and Frampton's general store, and the Niemes' drugstore.

Children from local farms would attend Artesia Grammar School and later ride a bus to Norwalk High School before Excelsior High School was built in 1925. On hot days after school, the children would gather near today's Carmenita Road and South Street for a dip in the reservoir at the Anthony ranch, which spread one hundred feet across and sixteen feet deep. Other childhood exploits weren't quite as wholesome. As Mrs. Nixon recalled, one Halloween night,

This aerial view of downtown Artesia, taken in the early 1900s, shows the Ponedel General Store at today's Pioneer Boulevard and 187th Street. The local institution was the place to shop for groceries, grain, and sundries. Images of America: Artesia 1875–1975.

The modern, brick Artesia Grammar School, nicknamed Pioneer School, replaced the region's old wooden schoolhouse in 1910. Damaged in the 1933 Long Beach earthquake, the school nevertheless stayed in operation until 1954. Images of America: Artesia 1875–1975.

The area's sugar beet crops were likely hauled to the nearby Los Alamitos Sugar Factory, shown ca. 1910. The complex, with company houses for workers, evolved into a Los Alamitos townsite. Courtesy of the University of Southern California, on behalf of the USC Specialized Libraries and Archival Collections.

The local climate provided the perfect conditions for growing grapes, as Artesians O. J. Thompson and George Frampton Sr. discovered. The duo ran a successful winery at the northeast corner of Pioneer and Artesia Boulevards. Images of America: Artesia 1875–1975.

"goblins" relocated a wagon to the roof of the Pacific Electric station and moved outhouses to the roofs of the buildings along Pioneer Boulevard—a story that has become legendary.

Mother Nature

Mother Nature would regularly play a little mischief of her own, dousing the area with winter storms. Before today's modern storm channels, low-lying Norwalk, Bellflower, and Artesia were especially known for flooding. Most winters, the area near Gridley Road between Del Amo Boulevard and South Street became a lake, and Coyote Creek regularly overflowed and flooded what is now Hawaiian Gardens.

After a severely wet winter in 1916, even one of the largest local rivers, the San Gabriel, overflowed. Life on the farms came to a halt, with crops inundated with water and the dirt roads an impassable mess. The Pacific Electric Red Cars, however, were able to remain in operation on their raised tracks, shuttling people and goods through even the worst weather. But despite its convenience, the rail line soon earned a few enemies. The Red Cars' raised tracks, it turned out, worked as a dam, regularly trapping the floodwaters. On this particularly

Longtime residents of Dairy Valley and Artesia regaled new generations for decades with stories of the area's notorious floods. The problem wouldn't be solved until county storm drains were installed in the 1960s. An awed resident surveys the damage in this undated photo.

33

Top: The Scott and Frampton building at Pioneer Boulevard and 187th Street was one of hundreds of buildings damaged by the Long Beach earthquake. The disaster, which struck on March 10, 1933, at 5:54 p.m., caused 102 fatalities and millions of dollars in damage. Images of America: Artesia 1875–1975.
Bottom: The brick Artesia Garage building, which once housed Ponedel General Store, sustained so much damage during the 1933 Long Beach earthquake that it could no longer be used. Throughout the region, spooked cows refused to go back in their barns again, fearing another jolt. Images of America: Artesia 1875–1975.

stormy night, a rising tide soon threatened the businesses along Pioneer Boulevard. As legend holds, a mysterious figure saved the town by blasting a piece of the track between Pioneer Boulevard and Studebaker Road with dynamite. The water level quickly subsided.

Such explosive tactics were no longer needed by the 1930s when large dams and reservoirs were built in the San Gabriel Mountains to capture dangerous runoff. "Spreading dams" were soon built to control the floods and allow some of the winter downpours to soak into the ground and replenish local wells. By the end of the 1960s, all of the local rivers and creeks had been lined in concrete, speeding the delivery of water to the ocean and away from neighboring properties.

Earthquakes, however, remained an uncontrollable force, and on March 10, 1933, Artesia residents were reminded of Mother Nature's power. Late in the afternoon, a 6.3 magnitude quake struck the nearby Newport-Inglewood fault. Had the earthquake occurred just a few years earlier when most of the region was devoted to ranching, the damage may have been negligible. But the population was now booming, with Long Beach and its neighboring towns filled with homes, businesses, and other structures. Nearly no consideration was given to earthquakes in those days, and most structures had been built using techniques common in the quake-free Midwest.

When the late afternoon temblor hit, the unreinforced brick-and-mortar buildings that dotted the landscape simply fell apart, killing more than 102 residents and causing more than $40 million in damage. Long Beach was devastated, and there was serious damage to buildings in Torrance, Garden Grove, and Compton. Several buildings in Artesia and Norwalk were so damaged they had to be torn down. Twenty-two local school buildings were destroyed, including Excelsior High School, which had been built just six years earlier at Pioneer and Alondra Boulevards. Once a showcase for the community, Excelsior lost its decorative portico and sustained other major damage. Artesia Grammar School was so badly damaged, it was replaced by another building on the same site, called Pioneer School.

Fortunately, students and faculty had all gone home before the late afternoon earthquake hit, a blessing that may have prevented hundreds of deaths and injuries. The state legislature acted immediately to pass the Field Act, which called for a strict new building code. All new schools, the act stated, must comply with a state building code and be carefully supervised.

Dairies

But floods and earthquakes would never be enough to overshadow the beauty of the Cerritos area, and its near-perfect climate and convenient location continued to attract new residents and entrepreneurs. It was directly after the Long Beach earthquake, in fact, that a stream of Dutch and Portuguese immigrants began to build Artesia into one of the nation's largest dairy capitals.

Over more than a century, hundreds of thousands of cows had roamed the land that is now Cerritos. But on the ranchos of the early 1800s, cows were typically prized only for their hides, meat, and tallow—not for their milk. Milking a longhorn cow on the ranchos was done only when necessary to obtain milk for an invalid or an infant. After all, as the story has been passed down, it was a three-man job to lasso the cow and try to hold it still long enough to extract a container full of milk.

Dairy farming became more desirable in the 1850s when American settlers moved to California with their taste for fresh milk, butter, and cheese. As the demand for dairy products grew, dairy farms sprung up first near San Francisco and later in Southern California. By the 1880s, there were several cheese factories and creameries in the Los Angeles Basin, with small local dairies supplying the milk. Most were concentrated on a belt from Compton through Buena Park.

The local dairy industry continued to grow through the 1920s, as did the need for milkers. With the promise of jobs, dozens of Portuguese immigrants who had worked at dairies in the San Joaquin Valley moved south to Los Angeles County. As the Los Angeles metropolitan area was filled in with housing, offices, shops, and industry, many dairies moved east, cementing the Artesia area as a dairy capital. The following decade, in the 1930s, hundreds of Dutch people—descended from generations of dairy farmers—were lured first to the Midwest and then to Southern California. They brought with them to Artesia the hands-on skills and expertise the dairy industry demanded.

Local dairies were, in short, milk factories. Gone were the rolling grassy pastures; instead, cows were farmed on small plots, averaging ten acres or fewer with about one hundred cows. The animals were now fed scientifically regulated fodder that included hay, cottonseed meal, copra, and other exotic food. Each cow was expected to produce her quota of twelve hundred gallons of milk a year, or a new cow would take her place. Fertilizer was a side business for many farmers, and local suppliers that sold hay and other dairy feed turned millions of dollars in profits.

Bottled immediately after milking

Top: Excelsior High School, the area's only high school for decades, was severely damaged just nine years after its 1924 construction. Fortunately, school was not in session when the 1933 Long Beach earthquake struck. Later, some local teachers created makeshift class-rooms in their garages. Images of America: Artesia 1875–1975.
Bottom: A local dairyman in a crisp white uniform oversees the production line at Mountain View Dairies, Inc. As the bottle lids boasted, the "guaranteed raw milk" was "produced and bottled on the farm."

This pastoral scene shows a typical Dairy Valley farm operation, with hundreds of black-and-white Holsteins housed in corrals. Cows would be milked by hand twice a day. Pictured is the future site of the Cerritos Towne Center.

Local motorists and farm truck drivers fueled up at the Koopman Gas Station, located at 12121 Artesia Boulevard just west of Norwalk Boulevard. This ca. 1939 photo shows the Koopmans and their eight children. Photo courtesy of Ted Koopman.

Dairying, by all accounts, was hard work, and there was little room for sentimentality. The cows had to be kept healthy and fed and milked regularly. Equipment had to be perfectly sterile. The cows worked seven days a week, fifty-two weeks each year, and the dairymen kept the same schedule. But the hard work paid off: the area's semi-marine climate was perfect for the cows and made possible phenomenal milk production. Some of the area's cows, in fact, produced three thousand gallons of milk a year—twice the national average. All totaled, the local dairy industry produced half a million gallons of milk monthly by the 1940s, for an annual profit of $61 million.

The Portuguese dairy workers, many of whom originated in the Azores islands, left an indelible mark on the region that continues to this day. The group established a warm community in the town of Artesia, with a fellowship hall forming the community's social center. It was here that the Portuguese Americans were able to retain their language, culture, and family ties. Meanwhile, the Dutch farmers created a "Little Holland" in the area, from Paramount to west Buena Park. Here, they could hear sermons in the Dutch Reformed churches, read newspapers from their native land, and enjoy a rich social and cultural life in their native language. When Queen Juliana and Prince Bernhard of the Netherlands toured the United States in 1952, they made a special visit to this area.

One of many Dutch-owned businesses in the region, Artesia's Ted Bouma Dairy served as host to Queen Juliana of the Netherlands in 1952. Queen Juliana is followed by Mrs. Bouma, Prince Bernhard, and Mr. Bouma. Images of America: Artesia 1875–1975.

The Divino Espirito Santo (D.E.S.) Hall in Artesia was built in 1935 and quickly became the place for meetings, community events, and celebrations throughout the Portuguese community. Known as "Portuguese Hall," the still-thriving center is located at 11903 Ashworth Street. Images of America: Artesia 1875–1975.

A Dairy Valley farmer leads his herd down a dirt road on a sunny Southern California day. Hay (shown on the right) and feed were also big commodities in the area, while manure was prized as fertilizer.

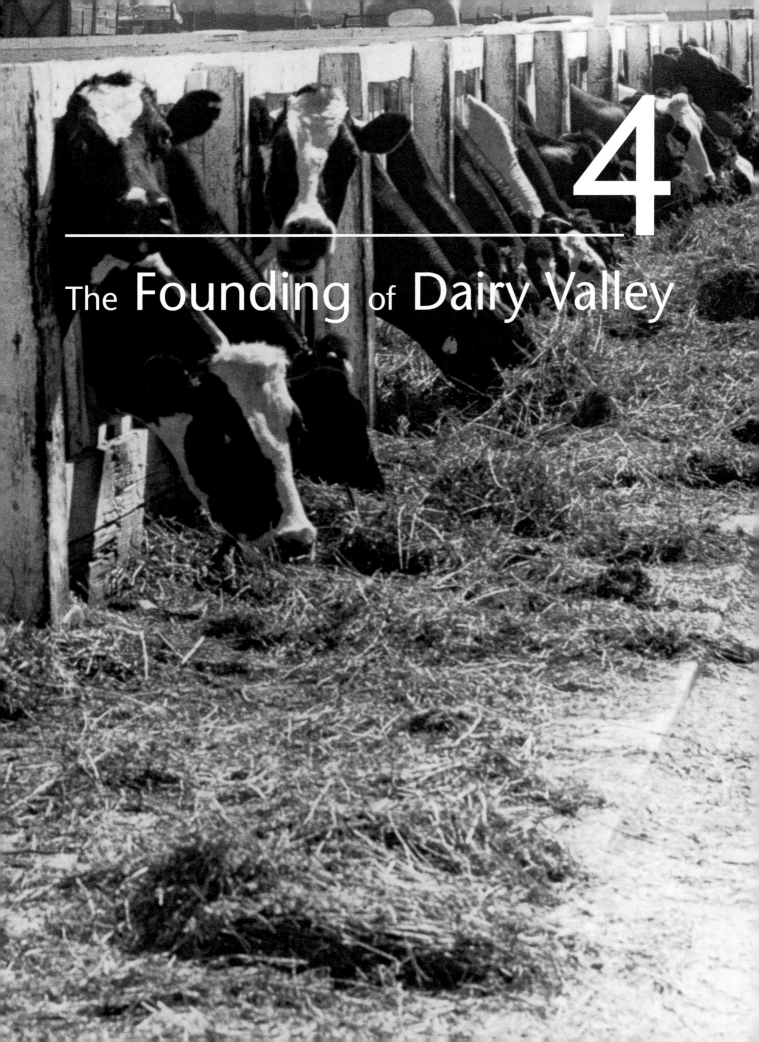

The Founding of Dairy Valley

4

The Building Boom

*B*y the 1940s, there was something in the air in Dairy Valley beyond the mooing of cows. The Los Angeles County housing boom had begun with a chorus of hammers, saws, and backhoes.

World War II had made Southern California an important industrial center, with thousands of workers moving to the area for good jobs in the local factories, shipyards, and plants that supplied the military. One of the area's major employers was the Douglas Aircraft Company, which opened in 1941 on the eve of World War II next to Daugherty Field in Long Beach. During the war, the facility produced more than thirty-one thousand aircraft for the U.S. Air Force, Navy, and Marine Corps, including bomber, cargo transport, and reconnaissance planes. The facility later went on to produce commercial jetliners. After the war, many of the local workers stayed, and thousands of returning veterans joined them on the assembly lines.

To accommodate this growing workforce, developers sped up production of dozens of tracts of homes in Long Beach, Artesia, and Norwalk. The most spectacular example was Lakewood, where a single developer bought 3,375 acres of farmland and, just as the last crops were being harvested, laid out 133 miles of paved streets. More than ten thousand homes were built in the first two years alone, using the most modern construction techniques. Power diggers trenched foundations in just under fifteen minutes, carpenters used automatic nailing machines and precut lumber, and conveyor belts carried shingles to the roofs. Priced at $7,000, the homes were snapped up by buyers who often took advantage of G.I. loans guaranteed by the Federal Housing Authority.

As Lakewood grew to the west, Norwalk settled in to the north, and Buena Park burgeoned to the east, Dairy Valley's farmers could see their area's rural roots start to wither.

Opened in 1941, the Douglas Aircraft Company's Long Beach facility covered nearly four hundred acres and delivered more than 15,400 commercial and military planes to agencies around the globe. Courtesy of Boeing.

One of the products of the Douglas Aircraft Company in Long Beach was the C-47 military version of the DC-3, which many say contributed to the Allied victory during World War II. Courtesy of Boeing.

Women were a significant part of the workforce at Douglas Aircraft during World War II, taking their places along the airplane production lines. "Rosie the Riveter" became an emblem for strength, determination, and freedom. Courtesy of Boeing.

Cities Rise from the Fields

As they took shape, neighboring cities also began to assert their independence. Throughout Southern California's rural past, most towns were recognized simply because they had a post office, school district, train station, or chamber of commerce. The county took care of street maintenance, police, and other services. But as local cities evolved from fields to suburbs, many took action to "incorporate," to meet the state's legal requirements for an independent city government.

In many cases, this led to land scuffles. When Lakewood's population exploded in the 1950s, for instance, this "instant city" became home to seventy-seven thousand people. While many assumed Lakewood would be annexed by its big-city neighbor, Long Beach, Lakewood leaders disagreed. They made arrangements to contract with Los Angeles County for many of the services that would normally put a new city into debt, including police and fire protection, libraries, and street maintenance. With this smart financial move, Lakewood incorporated in 1954.

Other cities took notice. In fact, so many local leaders were interested in the "Lakewood Plan" that the county set up an office to provide technical assistance. The state legislature also helped these growing burgs by passing the Bradley-Burns Act in 1956, which provided a 1 percent sales tax revenue for cities. With this financial assistance and the spirit of independence, forty-seven new cities were incorporated in the Los Angeles-Orange County area from 1954 to 1974.

A Push from Artesia

One of these cities was Artesia. By August 1951, Los Angeles County Ordinance 5800 had established the "Artesia Zoned District" south of Alondra Boulevard and between the San Gabriel River and Coyote Creek to the point

Amid Los Angeles County's post–World War II housing boom, photographer William A. Garnett created these gelatin silver prints of Lakewood in 1950, showing an artistic view of the construction. Courtesy of the J. Paul Getty Museum, Los Angeles.

For decades, children from many nationalities grew, studied, and played together at Artesia Grammar School, returning to their family farms each day after the final bell. The class of 1949 was the last to graduate from the brick building. Images of America: Artesia 1875–1975.

where the two streams meet. With help from Lakewood attorney Angelo Iacoboni, who had spearheaded his city's incorporation drive, the Artesia Chamber of Commerce embarked on a campaign in 1955 to incorporate the Artesia Zoned District and create one of the largest and wealthiest cities in Los Angeles County. The chamber staged an informal meeting at Mike's Café on Carson Boulevard in August to discuss the idea, inviting local dairymen Jim Albers, Frank Leal, Leslie Nottingham, and Albert Veldhuizen.

It was soon apparent, however, that this was not a "preliminary" meeting. Boundary papers and petitions were ready for distribution, calling for development that would not include poultry ranches or feed lots for cattle. Housing developments, the papers stated, would be sandwiched between the dairies.

The dairymen quickly got the message: cows wouldn't be welcome. Not only would the feed-lot ban place a burden on their dairy operations, there was no doubt the new homeowners would object to the dairies' odor and flies, as they had in neighboring cities. The plan not only threatened the dairymen's way of life, but also the multimillion-dollar businesses they planned to pass on to their children.

Through the 1950s, Dairy Valley remained one of the few communities where scenes like this were typical. When the city incorporated in 1956, the ratio of cows to people was thirty-to-one.

"We Were Satisfied": Life in Dairy Valley

Mr. and Mrs. M. Lanting and their three children first set foot in America in 1923, arriving from Holland by boat on the shores of Ellis Island. Mr. Lanting had been receiving letters about dairying opportunities, and he wanted a gainful future for his family. Upon arrival, the Lantings quickly caught a cross-country train to Bellflower, California, and Mr. Lanting went to work as a milker. Two years later, Mr. Lanting was offered a small dairy herd of his own in Clearwater (now Paramount), where he and his wife, Anne, did the hand-milking every day. There was no electricity, so they used kerosene lamps for light before dawn. It was a small operation but the beginning of their life in America.

By 1931, many dairies were setting up shop in the Artesia area, and Mr. Lanting was able to buy five acres and a small house on Gridley Road. He quickly added a milkhouse and corrals, built by hand. By now, the Lanting family included four children, including a little brunette named Annie.

Today, Ontario resident Annie (Lanting) Troost is a mother of six, grandmother of sixteen, and great-grandmother of twenty-seven, not to mention a former "first lady" of Cerritos and one of the best authorities on life in the early days of Dairy Valley.

Physically, Dairy Valley was a very different place in its early years, with pastures, strawberries, and sugar beets laid out as far as the eye could see, Mrs. Troost remembers. The land was quiet, stars twinkled at night, and the only smog came from the smudge pots—old rubber tires—neighbors burned to keep their orange crops from freezing on winter nights. "Traffic" consisted of families motoring over dirt roads to downtown Artesia for a stop at Tilton Drugstore, Parker Hardware, Frampton's Department Store, the public market, the local bank, or the five-and-dime.

"We were satisfied," Mrs. Troost remembers. "Coming out of the Depression, no one had anything to flaunt. Everyone was content with what they had. It was easy living."

As a student at Artesia Grammar School and, later, Excelsior High School, Mrs. Troost remembers friends of many nationalities—Portuguese, Dutch, Japanese, Mexican, and more—all dressed in navy skirts or slacks and crisp shirts with black collars. "Everybody got along, and there was no question about what to do after school," she said. "Everybody had to work; everybody had chores."

The boys would go home and help their fathers with the milking or tending the fields, while the girls would help their mothers with cooking and cleaning. Dairy work was particularly hard. The men of the family would get up at 1:00 a.m. to milk all of their cows by hand and then arrive home for breakfast before heading back to bed. They would rise again at 1:00 p.m. to milk the cows until suppertime. "It was a hard life," she said, "really two shifts, seven days a week." There was no fast food or

Young Annie Lanting poses in her Excelsior High School uniform, with its crisp black collar against a pure white shirt. She was a member of Excelsior's graduating class in 1938. Photo courtesy of Annie Troost.

restaurants, she noted, so the women would cook nearly round the clock to keep the dairy workers fed. On Sundays, dairy families would work a half-day to save time for church.

The children, however, always managed to find time for fun. Mrs. Troost remembers afternoons of ice skating or roller skating at the Hippodrome in Long Beach, family visits to the Long Beach Pike, and nickel rides on the Pacific Electric to Los Angeles. On rainy days, streets would flood, and adventurous boys would float on rafts down the thoroughfares. Everyone in town knew one another from church, school, or trips to town, so there was a great family atmosphere, she said. Holidays were big, with a yearly Artesia Fair, parade, carnival, and fireworks marking the Fourth of July. Schoolchildren looked forward to receiving free passes to the annual Los Angeles County Fair in Pomona, an eagerly anticipated event.

Now part of the city's Restaurant Row, the third and largest location of the Fred Troost & Sons Dairy operation once lined 183rd Street. This aerial photo was taken in 1961. Photo courtesy of Annie Troost.

In 1938, young Annie was part of the first graduating class from Excelsior High School to use the school's new auditorium, which replaced a building that had been destroyed by the 1933 earthquake. That year, Annie met a young Iowa college boy named Fred Troost at Artesia Reformed Church, and the couple was smitten. Married in 1941, the young couple started a family that would eventually include five sons and a daughter. With their savings, the Troosts invested in their first dairy of sixty cows on Pioneer Boulevard near today's 91 Freeway (where some of the Troost farm's original eucalyptus trees still stand).

Named Fred Troost & Sons, the operation moved in 1945 to a larger dairy on Orangethorpe and Grayland Avenues, supplying milk to Carnation Creamery. The family moved again in 1961, building a home on an existing dairy on 183rd Street, where the city's Restaurant Row stands today. (The 605 Freeway runs through what used to be the Troost corrals.) As industry and homes encroached on the area, Mr. Troost became a central figure in Dairy Valley's early government, serving as mayor in 1966–1967 and overseeing the city's development.

True to their heritage, the Troost boys have carried on the family's dairy dynasty by operating independently in New Mexico, Chowchilla, Bakersfield, and Oregon. Mr. Troost is deceased, and Annie is enjoying her golden years in Ontario and cherishing the memories.

Our Founding Fathers Meet

The very next day, the dairymen met with fellow Farm Bureau members at the Central Milk Producers Association offices on Pioneer Boulevard. Several pledged money to pay for an attorney, and paperwork was drawn up that would set the stage for incorporation of a separate, agriculturally based community carved from the Artesia Zoned District that would be named Dairy Valley.

There were similar stirrings just over Coyote Creek, where an area that would someday be known as La Palma incorporated itself as Dairyland to escape annexation by Buena Park. The city of Cypress, originally called Watertown, incorporated as Dairy City in 1956 to make clear its agricultural focus.

But the love of farming wasn't the only thing driving Dairy Valley's early leaders; they were also very astute entrepreneurs. As campaign literature would later state, the men were an average of forty-seven years old and had been successful local businessmen for twenty-five years. Their combined operations included 235 acres of valuable land, thirty-two hundred dairy cows, and twenty thousand chickens, and they tended to live in large, well-built homes, spending vacations in Europe. Most were on local, county, and state agricultural boards and served as trustees for their schools and churches. They were savvy in management and knew that if the area was correctly developed, it could only enhance their investments. When the dairies were ready to relocate, the men, of course, hoped to realize the greatest profit from their land.

Albert Veldhuizen, a Minnesota native of Dutch descent who lived with his wife and four sons on a Studebaker Road dairy, was elected chairman of the Dairy Valley committee. Other active members and future city council candidates included John Schoneveld from Iowa; Jacob "Jim" Albers and Louis Struikman, both born in Holland; Jack R. Bettencourt, originally from Massachusetts; and A. C. Pinheiro and Francisco C. De Mello, natives of the Portuguese Azores. Representing the poultry farmers were George Sperou, who was also an engineer, and Hal Rees, who had a career recording music for motion pictures before he established a poultry ranch with fifteen thousand birds.

Planned and incorporated as an "agricultural community," Dairy Valley would soon become a haven for cows. As homes encroached in neighboring cities, Dairy Valley's cows—and their owners—were able to stand their ground.

Milk made for a serious and profitable business for Dairy Valley's farmers. Cows were the vital part of the "assembly line," as shown in this photo taken in September 1959.

Dairy Valley's cows continued to produce millions of bottles of milk, not to mention dairy products like butter, ice cream, and cheese, throughout the 1950s. Assemblyline of Cartons, ca. 1940. Courtesy of the UCR/California Museum of Photography, Will Connell Collection, University of California at Riverside.

Cerritos Begins

Dairy Valley's incorporation was brought before voters in 1956, and the campaign was truly contentious. The dairymen worried that the Artesia boosters would prevail, with their four-to-one advantage among voters. The dairymen also feared that central Artesia, with an assessed value of $4 million, would hold power over the dairy area, valued at more than $18 million. They predicted that property and school taxes would inevitably rise, a special blow to the dairymen whose children most often attended private church schools.

Nine dairymen joined the slate of candidates for Dairy Valley's first city council, but they took the unheard-of step of campaigning as a bloc, taking out a full-page ad in the *Artesia News* to show their commitment to a common vision. "This is not a conventional political platform," they wrote. "These are the sincere pledges and guarantees of each and all of us." Promoting their idea for a new agricultural city, the dairymen promised not to "freeze things as they are now" but to encourage commercial development, clean industry, and one house per five acres. They promised a simple and economical government, with just two employees and no salary or expense accounts for the councilmen. What's more, the men promised lower county taxes and no city property taxes. As in Lakewood, the county would be contracted to provide services.

"There are only two choices for this area," their ad declared. "Do nothing on April 10th and within a year find yourself a forgotten, heavily taxed minority in someone else's town; or vote 'yes' on April 10th and take intelligent advantage of this first and last chance to have truly economical self-government here."

The men first sketched out a city that would include Artesia, Hawaiian Gardens, and a strip known as Monterey Acres, now part of Lakewood. But by election time, city boundaries had been scaled back. Political shenanigans, however, had not, and the tension continued to build. In one now-legendary move, the dairymen even arranged to buy up a new housing tract known as Artesia Crest to move in their milkers. This savvy move ensured that the new homes would be filled with voters friendly to the dairymen's cause.

The election was finally held on April 10, 1956. Although the results were close, 441 to 391, the dairy- and poultrymen prevailed. The Secretary of State approved the Articles of Incorporation, and Dairy Valley officially became a city at exactly 9:16 a.m. on Tuesday, April 24, 1956. Resembling a horseshoe encircling Artesia, the new City of Dairy Valley was home to 3,500 people, 32,000 cows, 83,000 chickens, 9,600 turkeys, and 105 acres of row crops, including fields of strawberries and sugar beets as far as the eye could see. The city's value was assessed at $26 million, and the first city budget was pegged at $33,190.

Top: *The scene has changed dramatically through the years near the corner of 183rd Street and Studebaker Road, shown here in the 1950s. Chevrolets, Hondas, and more at the Cerritos Auto Square have replaced cows.*

Bottom: *This tidy home at 13841 Artesia Boulevard was a typical residence for Dairy Valley's farm families. This photo was taken in April 1957.*

The names of the City of Dairy Valley's first organizers were already well known to the community, thanks to the signs that topped their family dairy operations. Jacob "Jim" Albers served on the first city council while A. C. Pinheiro lost a seat by just one vote.

Fred Troost, who served as mayor and councilmember on the Dairy Valley/Cerritos City Council in the 1960s, poses by one of the first aerial photos of the fledgling city.

Cerritos's Enduring Resident: Myrtle Franz

It was 1920 when five-year-old Myrtle Raine unpacked her bags in her new home on Orangethorpe Avenue (now South Street) in Dairy Valley. Her grandparents, Sid and Kate Beckworth, had arrived in 1911 from Iowa, eventually building a working ranch on Bloomfield Avenue. After a few years of cajoling, her grandparents convinced her parents, George and Anna Raine, to make the trek out from North Dakota, camping all the way with their five children and all their life's belongings in tow. The Raine family rented a place in Norwalk for six months before buying ten acres in 1920 near today's Cerritos Senior Center. A little girl named Pat Ryan (the future First Lady) lived next door, and Myrtle and she became fast friends, taking summer trips to the beach, sharing neighborhood babysitting duties, and walking the dirt roads to school. Pat, Myrtle, and Myrtle's older sister, Louise, became known as "the Three Musketeers."

Young Myrtle Raine and her sister, Louise, share a pair of roller skates as they zip around the family farm. Pictured behind the girls is a dirt road that was once called Orangethorpe Avenue (now South Street).

The Raine ranch included a small dairy of fifteen cows, a field of alfalfa for feed, and a "truck farm" that supplied cauliflower, potatoes, tomatoes, corn, and other vegetables to the markets in Long Beach and Los Angeles. Like most children of the day, Myrtle and her brothers and sisters worked the fields, milked the cows, and tended the house. "I was ironing Dad's shirts when I was seven years old," she remembers with a chuckle. "Hard work never hurt anyone."

The Raine children regularly wheeled ten-gallon cans of milk down to the road for pickup, often using the Ryan family's driveway or a ditch dotted with sheep droppings. With hoof-and-mouth disease rampant, the equipment and milk would need to be sterilized, and little Myrtle was charged with lighting and tending the fire. "I still like to light fires today," she laughs.

When their mother died in 1927, eleven-year-old Myrtle and her older sister, Louise, ran the household, just as her neighbor, Pat Ryan, had done after her mother's death two years earlier. Still dealing with their grief, the Raine children were delighted that school was cancelled one sunny day for the momentous street-lighting in downtown Artesia. They joined the entire community for a day of free hot dogs, games, and fun, and Myrtle remembers being touched by everyone's concern for her family.

By then, Myrtle had collected a large group of friends that included Ryan, Kathleen Hurley, whose father had started the Chamber of Commerce, Flo Gonsalves, whose family grew daffodils and other flowers on the neighboring ranch, and a young man, Elbert Borden, whose grandfather, Harvey Smith, had run a local creamery since 1905. Myrtle "thought he was cute," she laughs, and the couple married on February 21, 1936.

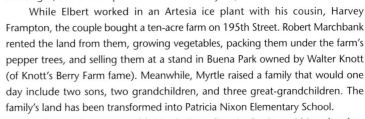

While Elbert worked in an Artesia ice plant with his cousin, Harvey Frampton, the couple bought a ten-acre farm on 195th Street. Robert Marchbank rented the land from them, growing vegetables, packing them under the farm's pepper trees, and selling them at a stand in Buena Park owned by Walter Knott (of Knott's Berry Farm fame). Meanwhile, Myrtle raised a family that would one day include two sons, two grandchildren, and three great-grandchildren. The family's land has been transformed into Patricia Nixon Elementary School.

Today, at ninety years old, Myrtle Franz lives in Cerritos within a few feet of her family's original ranch. She is a beloved personality and an eighty-year member of Artesia-Cerritos Methodist Church, a former Cub Scout and 4-H Club leader, and one of the original staff members of Artesia High School's cafeteria. What's more, she is a Neighborhood Watch captain and a repeat winner and judge of the Cerritos City Wide Pride program.

On her ninetieth birthday in 2005, Cerritos resident Myrtle Franz was presented with a medal for her years of service to her church, as well as a proclamation signed by one-time Cerritos mayor (and now Los Angeles County Supervisor) Don Knabe. She remains an active citizen.

"This city has changed so much, you wouldn't realize it's the same place," she says today. "I tell people I live in Cerritos, and they're so impressed. It's grown into a beautiful city. I'm very proud of it."

A Brand New City: the 1950s

The City of Dairy Valley—1956

During this momentous election, five men were chosen from the slate of nine candidates to serve as Dairy Valley's first city council. Jacob Albers was a sixteen-year dairyman whose five children and one thousand cows had the run of his forty-five-acre farm at 19510 Pioneer Boulevard. He had made a name for himself in the local farm and dairymen's associations, as well as the Artesia Rotary Club and the Christian Home for the Aged. Jack R. Bettencourt was a Massachusetts native and thirty-year dairyman, with a wife, six children, and 175 cows on his fifteen-acre farm at 16926 Marquardt Avenue. He had shown his leadership skills as a member of the Knights of Columbus and the local Farm Bureau. Hal Rees and his wife, a native of Catalina Island, had lived in the area for forty-six years. A veteran of the motion picture industry, he now devoted his time to his poultry farm and the Farm Bureau, Rotary Club, and Holy Family Church. The youngest member at thirty-six, Albert Veldhuizen was the father of "four husky sons" and the owner of a thirteen-acre farm with 475 cows at 16330 Studebaker Road. He, too, was an active Rotarian and member of the Farm Bureau and Artesia Reformed Church. Louis Struikman, who had won over A. C. Pinheiro by just one vote, was a native of Holland who lived with his wife and son on a thirty-acre farm with seven hundred cows at 13841 Artesia Boulevard. He was also a familiar face at his church and a longtime member of the local Milk Control Board.

A Dairy Valley Holstein poses with her day-old calf in September 1959. Each cow was required to have a calf each year to maintain the quality and quantity of her milk. Calves were immediately sold.

The triumphant group wasted not a second, holding their first community meeting on election night at the Carmenita School auditorium, the only room in town big enough to hold an audience. Bettencourt was elected Dairy Valley's first mayor, and William "Bill" Cecil, business manager for Central Milk Sales at 17032 S. Pioneer Boulevard, was named temporary city manager. Joy D. Horn was hired as city clerk and treasurer, for an annual salary of $350. Soon after, the new city council acquired a $3,000 loan from a local feed company to pay the new staff members and to set up a temporary city hall at the Central Milk Sales office. (City offices moved later that year to 11810 E. 186th Street.)

One of the provisions of the April 10 election was that Dairy Valley would have a city manager form of government. With this structure, the citizens elect a city council to set policy, the mayor serves as chairperson, and a city manager is hired to prepare the budget, oversee daily operations, and advise the council. When Bill Cecil returned to his old job at Central Milk Sales in September, the council quickly chose Mayrant D. "Mac" McKeown as Dairy Valley's first permanent city manager. Just beginning his career at age thirty-three, McKeown held degrees in public administration from Long Beach State College and the University of California at Los Angeles. He was assisted by Margaret Bengel, who had replaced Mrs. Horn as city clerk and treasurer, and later by Agnes Hickey, who became the official city clerk in April 1957 and remained in that position for twenty-four years.

Daily Operations

The newly minted leaders quietly went about the business of running their new city, considering development requests for new businesses and housing, instituting an annual "Fix Up, Clean Up" program, setting up a fertilizer cooperative, and dispatching a safety team to inspect the city's four private swimming pools. They put their stamp on a number of new laws banning illegal trash dumping, abandoned cars, and calf-skinning operations that were the scourge of many rural areas. They launched the city's recreation department, hiring John List to supervise the Carmenita School playground for $1.75 an hour.

Meanwhile, they enlisted the county's help to pave Dairy Valley's dirt roads. County engineers estimated it would take $3 million to transform Dairy Valley's rustic thoroughfares into "civilized" condition, and work soon began to convert Pioneer Boulevard, South Street, and Artesia Boulevard into modern, paved, two-lane roads. Most of the other streets were left unpaved.

Residents, meanwhile, had grown tired of the area's notorious annual flooding. The Coast Guard had evacuated many from their sodden homes during the heavy storms of January 1952, and memories were still fresh. After any heavy

Top: City Clerk Agnes Hickey swears in members of Dairy Valley's first Planning Commission, charged with laying out the future of the brand-new city.
Bottom: While local drivers had become accustomed to kicking up clouds of dust as they drove through Dairy Valley, leaders decided that their new city was ready for modern paved roads. Pictured is the intersection of 183rd Street and Studebaker Road. Curbs, sidewalks, and other niceties would have to wait.

Streets in Artesia and Dairy Valley were notorious for their flooding before modern storm channels were built. After heavy rains, residents would commute with rowboats and rubber boots, while motorists would carefully navigate through roads-turned-rivers. Images of America: Artesia 1875–1975.

Residents stand ankle-deep in cold water after heavy storms flood Artesia's downtown. Artesians later helped lobby for better drainage, securing funding for the Los Angeles County Artesia-Norwalk Storm Drain System. Images of America: Artesia 1875–1975.

rains, most residents assumed Gridley Road would be a lake. Local dairymen sometimes aggravated the problem by erecting levees around their own corrals, forcing floodwaters onto their neighbors, who were growing weary of these tactics. The situation improved considerably by 1957 when a much-needed drainage ditch was built from 183rd to South Street and later extended to Coyote Creek. The San Gabriel River and Coyote Creek were tamed a few years later when the Army Corps of Engineers lined them with concrete.

Neighborly Disagreements

McKeown and the council also faced their share of manmade challenges, including ongoing tussles with neighboring cities over land. In their 1956 campaign advertising, the council candidates had pledged, "We are not figuring on joining the scramble to annex new land. If folks with a common interest adjoining Dairy Valley want to come in, they will be welcome, but you won't find us out grabbing new areas!"

But this easygoing attitude soon took a back seat to pride and finances, and the council worked hard to preserve the land they felt was rightfully Dairy Valley's. Lakewood and Bellflower, for instance, had expected to annex the dairies west of the San Gabriel River, while Santa Fe Springs and Norwalk hoped to expand their industrial areas southward. After several court battles, Dairy Valley gained acreage, and the city's western boundary was set at Palo Verde Street. In one case, however, the city council wasn't so reluctant to give up land. When nondairy residents of Artesia Crest, near Pioneer and Del Amo, organized a

The queen of Artesia-Dairy Valley poses with Councilmembers Frank Leal, Fred Troost, Jim Albers, and Tony Cordeiro. Photo courtesy of Mrs. Annie Troost.

County Supervisor Frank Bonelli (with shovel) joins the festivities as the city lays out new water infrastructure. He is pictured with members of the Dairy Valley City Council and staff. Photo courtesy of Mrs. Annie Troost.

Mayor Fred Troost takes time off from his civic duties to give city officials a tour of his dairy operations. Photo courtesy of Mrs. Annie Troost.

The Cerritos College campus bookstore buzzes with activity during the first days of class in the late 1950s. Courtesy of the Cerritos College Office of Public Affairs.

movement to recall the city council, the dairymen managed to keep their seats, and the tract was swiftly annexed to Lakewood.

At the same time, Dairy Valley's city council battled with trustees of Cerritos College, who had set their sights on the corner of Alondra Boulevard and Studebaker Road, farmland they judged to be safe from flooding. Dairy Valley's leaders, however, felt the development would set a precedent that would threaten their rural zoning. The college would also grow and demand more dairy land, they predicted, and it would attract staff and students who would require housing. The matter was settled out of court when property was ceded to the city of Norwalk and an eight-foot-high, twelve-hundred-foot-long wall was built to mark the boundary. (At the same time, Dairy Valley's city council easily passed a request by Bellflower Christian School to build Valley Christian High School on Artesia Boulevard.) Today, while Cerritos College has a Norwalk address, much of the campus is situated in Cerritos.

After many adjustments, in 1957, the city of Dairy Valley was finally settled at 8.9 square miles. With dairies relocating to this new agricultural center, the city soon boasted four hundred dairies with over one hundred thousand cows, producing more than $80 million in milk products each year.

A Charter City with an Official City Hall

Dairy Valley continued to evolve into the 1960s, with voters opting to switch from a "general law" city to a "charter" city in November 1958, gaining broader powers and local zoning control. City Manager McKeown, meanwhile, earned a pay raise from $400 to $850 a month, plus accolades for a string of accomplishments. He managed to secure Dairy Valley's annexation of the area's only car dealership, S & J Chevrolet, as well as Olin Krum's Pioneer Mills, Barr Lumber, Jack Stansbury Dairy Supplies, and other prime businesses near Pioneer Boulevard and South Street. Sales tax, state funds, and even billboard rentals helped boost the city's coffers.

Dairy Valley's neighbor, Artesia, incorporated in 1959 with 1.62 square miles and ten thousand residents. Cerritos College opened that July, providing a central junior college campus for classes that were once held at night at local

This 1950s aerial photo shows the Troost family dairy lands, dotted with cows, along 183rd Street. Photo courtesy of Mrs. Annie Troost.

Dairy Days on Bloomfield Avenue

John and Emma Barbaria first emigrated from Portugal's Azores Islands via New York in 1945 and settled in Norwalk, where John was hired as a milker for J. C. Panherio. As legend holds, Mr. Panherio liked the family so much that he offered them $10,000 to buy a dairy of their own. The Barbarias jumped at the offer and bought a ten-acre plot that would soon house more than five hundred cows.

On the left side of the photo is the Benjendorf hay company that delivered provisions to many of the local dairies. On the right is the Hatanaka egg ranch, whose owner, Harry Hatanaka, built a home across the street that reportedly still stands today.

Over the years, the Barbaria property has been handed down through the generations. As housing tracts and warehouses surrounded the land in the 1970s, grandsons Dan, Larry, and Richard Barbaria took over the family business and developed their own warehouses under the name Barbaria Commercial Properties, LLC.

This 1948 photo shows the newly opened Barbaria Dairy at 16230 Bloomfield Avenue, between 166th Street and Alondra Boulevard. Photo courtesy of Linda Bruinsma for the Barbaria family.

high schools. The Santa Ana Freeway (Interstate 5) opened to motorists near the city's northern boundary, and Dairy Valley's great expanses invited creative ideas for development. At one time, Dairy Valley was suggested as the site for the Dodgers' new baseball stadium and as a perfect location for a small plane airport. Alas, the Los Angeles Airport Commission disagreed.

The community did agree, however, on the need for an official city hall, and on June 11, 1960, city officials celebrated the opening of a modern structure of green stucco and decorative blocks at 19400 Pioneer Boulevard. Designed by an architect friend of McKeown's, sketched free-of-charge over a spaghetti dinner, the building housed offices for city staff and a council meeting room that seated up to seventy people. The building was landscaped with a small lawn and stately palm trees. At the same time, on McKeown's advice, Dairy Valley pulled out of the county library district to save $20,000 a year. But on learning that the city was required by the state to provide library services, McKeown brought a shelf full of books from home, setting up Dairy Valley's first "public library."

To boost revenue, the city began charging a range of business license fees, from $5 a year for cow and chicken farms up to $100 annually—plus ten cents per barrel—from an oil company they hoped would strike "gold" north of 166th Street. The Producers' Livestock Marketing

Los Angeles County Supervisor Frank Bonelli was a featured speaker at Dairy Valley City Hall's groundbreaking. The stage was set up next to the iconic row of palm trees that once lined Pioneer Boulevard.

Association relocated from Los Angeles to the corner of South Street and Carmenita Road, and a fee-per-head on animal sales gave a much-needed boost to the city's purse. Meanwhile, a ten-cents-per-head tax on hog sales helped ward off loud, smelly hog farms, but the fee attracted national attention and a lawsuit from the hog farmers' association. (The council later agreed to change the tax.) McKeown was lured away to Paramount with an offer of $20,000 per year, and William Stark took his place.

National Attention

By now, Dairy Valley's successful experiment in agricultural zoning had become a local marvel, attracting even national attention. Feature articles were published in the *Los Angeles Herald Examiner, California Farmer,* the U.S. government's Yearbook of Agriculture for 1963, and even a newspaper in Montreal, Canada. The story of Dairy Valley was later featured in a U.S. Department of Agriculture publication and became a staple in textbooks on urban planning read by college students across the country.

Shovels festively painted for the occasion mark the groundbreaking of Dairy Valley's first city hall on December 21, 1959.

Dozens of revelers celebrated the June 11, 1960, dedication of Dairy Valley's modern city hall with a springtime feast. The ladies wore dresses and pumps while the men donned suits and fedoras.

Dairy Valley's first city hall at 19400 Pioneer Boulevard, between 195th Street and South Street, was designed by an architect friend of the city manager's, sketched gratis over a spaghetti dinner. The building was later demolished, and the land was developed into homes.

This aerial photo, taken by Spence Air Photos of Los Angeles, shows the northeast portion of Dairy Valley in 1963. While the city remained an agricultural haven, residential development burgeoned just outside city limits.

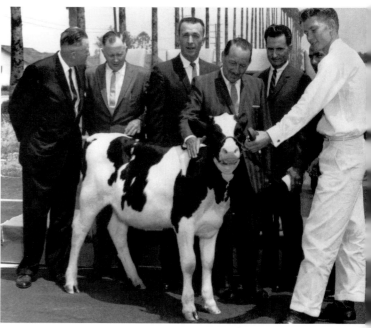

Los Angeles County Supervisor Frank Bonelli was later presented with a calf. He is pictured with Dairy Valley City Councilmembers (left to right) Louis Struikman, Jim Albers, Alex Moore, Joe Gonsalves, Frank Leal, and an unidentified calf herder.

Remembering the Lazy L Ranch

Cows weren't the only animals in Dairy Valley. Mel and Stella Long purchased the Lazy L Horse Ranch in 1949 at Rural Route 2, Norwalk, California—a plot of land that once served as a beet farm. Eventually pegged as 16708 Shoemaker Road, the ranch address also read Artesia and Dairy Valley before the post office finally settled on Cerritos.

It was here that daughter Linda (Long) Bruinsma and her sisters, Gerrie and Cheryl, enjoyed an idyllic childhood, riding ponies down the dirt road that was 166th Street, stopping at the country store on the way to Carmenita School, and hanging out at the drive-through dairy on the corner of Alondra Boulevard and 166th Street licking summer ice-cream cones. Bruinsma also remembers regular visits from "John the bakery man," who came with his truck filled with fresh pastries and breads.

Once located at Rural Route 2 in Norwalk, the Lazy L Ranch was assigned to several cities before Cerritos. The ranch also began with a ten-party phone line with the Underhill prefix. Each time a change was made, the Long family reprinted their business cards. Photo courtesy of Linda Bruinsma.

"We had a simple, quiet lifestyle in our city growing up," she said. "We knew all of the neighbors. Most of the local kids went from kindergarten to twelfth grade together, [and] many of us are still friends today."

At the Lazy L Ranch, the Long family watched over more than one hundred horses, providing boarding, training, and riding lessons, as well as animals for the movies. As in most farm families, the Long children helped with the chores, growing vegetables, milking the family cow, and watching over a flock that included a pig, a steer, chickens, llamas, and peacocks. Linda learned to drive a tractor at the age of ten and helped pump water from a well on the property—"the best water you could ever taste!" she reports. Stella and Linda Long were also regulars in the local parades, riding horseback.

As tract homes moved in, the Long family saw "more paved roads, stop signs and lights, more students at school, new stores, and more cars on the road," Bruinsma said. Before the 91 Freeway was built, her father asked her to take photos of the dirt path that would soon be a freeway. "I was thinking, 'what a waste of film,'" she laughs. "Well, I did as he said."

The Long family lived on the ranch until 1974, when it was sold to be developed as a school.

Azeke was the official greeter at the Lazy L Ranch in Cerritos, owned by Mel and Stella Long. Photo courtesy of Linda Bruinsma.

Stella Long, on Azeke, rides horseback in the 1963 Artesia parade. Her family's Lazy L Ranch raised Arabian, Thoroughbred, Peruvian Paso, and Shetland stallions. Photo courtesy of Linda Bruinsma.

A Changing City with a New Name: the 1960s

6

Start of an Exodus

This new "agricultural city" was clearly a success. But as much as Dairy Valley's first leaders wanted to preserve the city's rural roots, time marched on, and soon so did the cows. With many of the area's original dairymen retiring or relocating to Chino or California's Central Valley, by 1962, Dairy Valley's dairies had been reduced by nearly half—to 240—with 53,000 cows producing 217,000 gallons of milk a day. Construction was now underway on two freeways—Interstate 605 and State Route 91—that would cut across the city, displacing thirty-two dairies and the fertilizer cooperative, but making the area more desirable for commuting homeowners.

As milk production slowed and thousands of new homes took shape in spotless new suburbs throughout the county, Dairy Valley residents turned their gaze toward "greener pastures." During a special election in July 1963, proponents of a citywide zoning change suggested that it was "Time to Cash In" on rising land prices, encouraging the city's dairies to move elsewhere to make room for suburban development.

The ads were certainly enticing. One memorable full-page piece in the *Artesia Advocate* showed dramatic "then" and "now" illustrations of the city. "Then" showed a hand gripping a fistful of dirt, while the picture opposite showed a well-dressed family gazing at a futuristic city of homes, industry, bullet trains, skyscrapers—even a rocket ship. "Today, your Dairy Valley property can be profitably sold or highly developed," the ad read, "if it is properly re-zoned!" The ad went on to warn of poor widows who would be forced to sell their husbands' fields for half to one-third their potential value. Housing authorities and real estate professionals agreed that pricing for acreage was peaking, the ad cautioned, so much so that the average home price could rise to

While Dairy Valley's farms were dwindling by the early 1960s, the city remained the site of the Los Angeles Producers Stock Yard, which hosted frequent auctions at 13131 E. South Street, east of Shoemaker Road. This photo was taken in April 1962.

"$25,000 MINIMUM. How many families of any age group can afford a house of this cost? This can cause the building of homes to be reduced dramatically," the ad warned, "causing over-inflated land prices to collapse."

But voters didn't respond well to these dire warnings. Despite any financial opportunities, residents weren't yet ready to bid farewell to their community's bovine past, and the measure was soundly defeated.

Residents were receptive, however, to minor zoning changes that promised a boost to the city treasury. It had become increasingly expensive to oversee Dairy Valley's progress, and the city budget had topped $260,000 by 1963. Leaders hoped that new retail centers and a light manufacturing area along the city's major thoroughfares would help bring not only services but also sales tax and

Of the more than two hundred dairies that prospered in Dairy Valley, only one remains today: the Jersey Gold Dairy drive-up store at 19922 Pioneer Boulevard. Owner Pete Vande Witte, a descendant of Dutch farmers, helped the previous owner run the Jersey Gold bottling line that once operated behind the store.

business license revenue to the city. To help bring this idea to fruition, the Dairy Valley Chamber of Commerce was founded on July 2, 1963, and John Corcoran was hired full-time to attract new businesses to town. The city's very first shopping center opened soon after at the corner of Pioneer and Del Amo boulevards, featuring an Alpha Beta grocery store, the TG&Y variety store, and several smaller shops.

Increasingly proud of their new city, Dairy Valley residents held tightly to their borders. In one case, Dairy Valley leaders quashed an idea set forth by neighboring Artesia, which hoped to annex Hawaiian Gardens, a little town south of Dairy Valley that had gotten its name from a popular soft drink stand that once stood at the corner of Carson and Norwalk boulevards. Artesia and Hawaiian Gardens could only be connected if Dairy Valley allowed a corridor to be cut through the bottom of its "horseshoe." The plan was rejected, and Hawaiian Gardens later incorporated on its own in 1964 with just under a half square mile of land.

Mayor Fred Troost, center, helps with the 1963 installation of officers for the Dairy Valley Chamber of Commerce. Pictured with Troost (left to right) are Adrian Boer, Joe Gorzeman, Henry De Bie, Bill Vierra, Ray Hansen, and Jake Cleo.

Local residents celebrated the opening of the city's first shopping center at Pioneer and Del Amo Boulevards. By the 1970s, the Alpha Beta chain boasted more than two hundred grocery stores and fifty Alphy's coffee shops throughout the west. The company merged with Ralphs in the late 1980s.

City Councilmembers Fred Troost (far left) and Louis Struikman (far right) offer a tour to the California Dairy Princess (ca. 1965–1968).

Model cows flank a cake baked for the City of Dairy Valley's eighth anniversary in 1964. Pictured from left are Councilmember Louis Struikman and his wife, Alice, Mrs. Lois Leal, Mayor Pro Tem Alex Moore, Mayor Frank Leal, Councilmember Fred Troost, Mrs. Kenneth Penrose of Artesia, and Councilmember J. N. Albers.

A Master Plan

In cases like these, Dairy Valley's residents held on tenaciously to their land, their ideals, and their pastoral way of life throughout the early 1960s. But as neighboring cities continued to grow around them, it became clear that development in Dairy Valley was inevitable. What was needed, they decided, was a plan. If the city was destined to grow, leaders and residents alike wanted to ensure that its valuable dairy fields were put to the best possible use.

The city hired experts Louis Turrini and Kenneth Outwater from Robert H. Grant and Company to prepare its first Master Plan in October 1964, which described Dairy Valley as "the last large unurbanized region in the metropolitan area." At the same time, to make Dairy Valley more desirable for future development, the city took out $3 million in municipal bonds to pay for a new water system that included modern twenty- and twenty-four-inch lines and, later, a six-million-gallon reservoir at the corner of Marquardt Avenue and 166th Street. The system was later christened when Mayor Jim Albers smashed a quart of milk across one of the freshly laid concrete pipes.

These upgrades were finished just in time. By the following year, in 1965, a county reappraisal had doubled Dairy Valley's property taxes, making the city a very expensive place to operate a dairy. Once again, the idea of changing Dairy Valley's zoning was presented to the city's voters. This time, the majority supported a change, with a vote of 440 to 324. Dairy Valley's zoning was officially redesignated from agricultural to residential.

Housing developers wasted no time. Shortly after the election, paperwork was filed at City Hall requesting permission to build one thousand new homes. The first tract to open, called Stardust Homes, offered beautiful abodes priced from a modest $24,000 to $30,000 to entice sturdy, middle-class buyers. To mark the momentous grand opening, Mayor Fred Troost presented a black-and-white cow statue to Mr. and Mrs. Marvin Chenevert, who, with their five children, were the very first residents to move into a Dairy Valley subdivision, at 19203 Crossdale Avenue.

Top: Modern water mains, sewer lines, and storm drains helped lay the foundation for a modern city, attracting new residents and businesses. Here, Dairy Valley water system improvements are under construction in June 1964.
Bottom: Today, the Cerritos Water Division serves sixteen thousand connections and maintains three wells, 181 miles of transmission lines, 1,646 fire hydrants, and three reservoirs holding twenty-four million gallons of water. The city's original reservoir, pictured here, at 166th Street and Marquardt Avenue is still in service.

This 1960s-era aerial photo looking east shows Bloomfield Avenue in the foreground and 183rd Street to the right, with the new 91 Freeway cutting across the landscape and subdivisions slowly filling in the cow pastures to the east.

Mayor Fred Troost (left) and Councilmember Louis Struikman (far right) congratulate Mr. and Mrs. Marvin Chenevert and their five children as they move into the very first tract home in Dairy Valley in 1966.

Planning for an "Explosion"

Following the Chenevert family's lead, new homebuyers began arriving in droves, bringing with them great hopes for the future, pride in their new community, and rows of fresh-faced children trailing behind them. Dairy Valley's leaders quickly decided that the community's growing families needed a better place to play than in the streets. Richard Bigler Associates was hired to prepare a comprehensive, long-range plan for parks and recreation. The document mapped out a solid plan for providing neighborhood parks citywide, with a range of carefully chosen amenities—from baseball fields to playgrounds to shady picnic grounds. The plan also called on the city to use every financing program available to purchase vacant land for future parks. With this plan in place, through the next decades, Dairy Valley boasted the highest number of parks per capita of any city in the area.

At the same time, while generations of Dairy Valley children had been served for nearly a century by their local schools, it soon became apparent that the community needed one central school district to oversee its educational direction. In 1965, voters agreed on a plan to combine three smaller districts into one, and the Artesia district (founded in 1875), Bloomfield district (founded in

Top: *In this June 1964 photo, carpenter Bill Crawford works on the framing of Dairy Valley's new Richard Gahr High School at 11111 Artesia Boulevard between Studebaker and Gridley Roads.*

Left: *Dairy Valley followed "the Lakewood Plan" and contracted many services from Los Angeles County. Future California governor George Deukmejian (left) joined Los Angeles County Supervisor Frank Bonelli in dedicating Cerritos Fire Station No. 35 in 1970.*

1885), and Carmenita district (founded in 1902) merged to become the ABC Unified School District. That year, Carver Elementary, Tetzlaff Junior High, and Gahr High School were completed. In addition, the district drew up plans that called for twenty-eight elementary schools, six junior high schools, and three high schools to meet the needs of what they expected to be a population explosion.

Our First General Plan

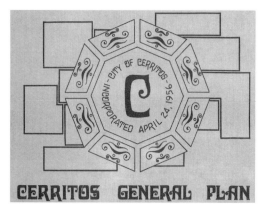

Top: The Los Angeles County Sheriff's Department has a long history of service to the Dairy Valley/Cerritos community, dating back to the city's incorporation. Sheriff's deputies have continued an active, community-based approach to serving residents and business owners.

Bottom: The Cerritos General Plan laid out a bright (and specific) future for this growing city. Available at Cerritos City Hall, Cerritos Library, and on the city's web site, the document is updated regularly to ensure the city's continued success.

While school district officials planned for new campuses, Dairy Valley's city staff continued to map out the best possible uses for the community's dairy fields. Stanley A. Morgan was hired as assistant to the city manager, and William Stookey, an MIT and Caltech graduate who had worked on the city's $3 million water main, was hired as the city's chief engineer. Local assemblyman Joe Gonsalves, who had himself grown up in Dairy Valley and served on the city council, secured a $33,000 state grant to prepare Dairy Valley's first General Plan.

California State Law requires every city to adopt a General Plan to provide a framework for the long-term physical development of the community. But for Dairy Valley, as for many other cities, the General Plan was much more than just a legal document. It served as a vision for the community's future, a firm statement of its character, and a tangible plan for preserving and promoting the city's heritage, values, and objectives.

City leaders professed that they didn't want Dairy Valley to be like so many other new communities that had mushroomed without direction. They wanted to attract solid, middle-class homeowners. They wanted all of the utility lines to be buried, with no poles and lines to mar the city's skyline. They wanted an abundance of parks, big community centers, and smaller neighborhood playgrounds within walking distance of every family. And they wanted a variety of commercial centers and an unobtrusive industrial center tucked away from residential neighborhoods.

When it was finalized in 1971, the comprehensive General Plan laid out a vision for a beautiful city with a balanced economy that would provide a safe, attractive home for growing families. Nearly half of the city's land was allocated for residential development, another 18 percent was dedicated to commercial, industrial, and professional uses, and the remaining third was designated for schools, parks, flood control facilities, utilities, public streets, and government buildings. More importantly, the General Plan called for a progressive city with deep respect for the environment and a lush, park-like setting that would give the community a unique beauty. Through the following years, City Councilmembers Dennis G. Bradshaw, Frank D. Lee, Barry A. Rabbitt, James S. Reddick, and Robert J. Witt were instrumental in overseeing the city's change from dairy land to a beautifully planned community.

Today, the Cerritos General Plan is much more complex, addressing land use, circulation, housing, conservation, open space, noise, and safety. But since its adoption in 1971, the document has been revised just twice, in 1988 and 2003, building on the accomplishments of the past, addressing the challenges of the future, and preserving the city's enduring values.

A New Name for a Modern City

While this planning was underway, Dairy Valley's leaders also decided to face their future with a brand new name. This modern suburban community, of course, could no longer be called Dairy Valley. As neighboring Dairyland remade itself as "La Palma" and Dairy City transformed itself into "Cypress," Dairy Valley's Chamber of Commerce began pushing for a more contemporary name for their master-planned community.

The Chamber's commercial and industrial committee set to work preparing a list of suggestions. "Los Coyotes" would have been a fitting tribute to the area's first name, Chamber members felt, but the name didn't quite have the sophisticated connotation they were looking for. Likewise, "Freeway City" was briefly considered, but it too lacked the "classy image" Chamber members and city leaders hoped for.

"Cerritos" was suggested as a name that would link the city with the successful junior college that was now becoming well known throughout Southern California. Cerritos also conjured up romantic images of the old California rancho days, city leaders felt. Historical accuracy, however, it didn't have. Rancho los Cerritos was actually the westernmost part of the old Nietos rancho, all of which was west of the San Gabriel River, with its eastern boundary at Bellflower Boulevard. Alas, none of the old Rancho los Cerritos even touched Dairy Valley. What's more, Abel Stearns had originally spelled the name "Sierritos," meaning "little hills," in a survey map in 1834—but what hills he was referring to remains a mystery. Voters didn't seem to care about these technicalities.

Sister Cities Abroad

Representatives from the city of Loreto, Mexico, accepted the gift of a fire truck from the City of Cerritos in May 1999.

With a twenty-hour trip to the town of Itapetinga, Brazil, in December 1964, Cerritos Councilman Frank Leal and his wife helped develop a lasting relationship with Dairy Valley's very first "Sister City."

The only Portuguese-speaking member of the city council, Leal was greeted by a huge welcome banner and a thousand cheering fans when he reached the city of thirty-seven thousand residents in Bahia, Brazil. Mr. and Mrs. Leal were paraded through the streets and then offered a tour of the city and gracious accommodations in the mayor's mansion.

The couple was later awakened at four o'clock in the morning by a marching band and fireworks before they were whisked off to a flag-raising ceremony, a parade with the governor of Bahia, and the dedications of Dairy Valley Park and a new emergency medical center. The local Brazilian Rotary and Lions clubs hosted evening banquets, and a choir concert was interrupted by a standing ovation when the Leals arrived.

Cerritos reciprocated four years later in October 1968, when a contingent arrived from the city of Itapetinga, including four Brazilian mayors, interpreters, and officials from the United States State Department. Cerritos-Artesia service clubs and the Chamber of Commerce lavished the visitors with dinners and presentations and named four Cerritos streets in their honor: Itapetinga, Bahia, Espinheira (the mayor's name), and San Salvador, the home city of a visiting city planner.

Banchaio, Taiwan, became the city's Sister City in March 1986, enjoying an official nine-day visit from Councilman Daniel Wong and members of a new Sister City Foundation. Banchaio leaders later visited Cerritos, presenting a beautiful vase that was displayed at Cerritos Library. In 2005, a delegation from Banchaio, including Mayor Hung-Lu Chang, visited Cerritos and enjoyed a tour of the city with members of the city council.

In July 1999, Cerritos formalized another lasting relationship with the city of Loreto, Mexico, a beautiful seaside community of seventy-five hundred residents in Baja California. The two cities had been united in tragedy by the 1986 air disaster that took lives from both communities. A volunteer group, dubbed the Friends of Loreto, remained in contact with the town, providing assistance and donations that included a fire truck and firefighting equipment. At the same time, the city joined Sister Cities International, a group created by President Eisenhower in 1956 to promote peace and goodwill worldwide.

"Cerritos" was the resounding winner during a city election on January 10, 1967.

Growing Better with Age

Just a little over a decade after the city was first incorporated, Cerritos had become a different place entirely. The acres of feedlots, strawberries, and chicken farms had begun to make way for suburban neighborhoods. By April 1968, thirty-one new tracts were either completed or underway, with more than two thousand new homes dotting the landscape. Huge construction crews were putting the finishing touches on the 605 and 91 freeways, crossing Cerritos in each direction and giving the city a convenient, central locale between Los Angeles and Orange counties. Enormous drainage, water, and sewer projects were underway, some connecting with systems in Norwalk, La Palma, and Lakewood. First Lady Patricia Nixon attended the groundbreaking in 1969 of a little park located on the farm where she had lived as a child. The family house later became a museum and recreation center.

The first section of the Artesia Freeway (CA-91) was dedicated in June 1968, complete with a skit starring "Daisy, The Educated Cow," who was trained by her owner, Mayor Pro Tem Tony Cordeiro, to chew through the grand-opening ribbon. This appeared to be one of the last of the "cute cow" presentations. In the months to come, many of the area's ninety thousand cows were loaded onto trucks and shipped off to new pastures.

As the cows headed east into the horizon, starting an exodus that would last into the next decade, Cerritos was swept up in a spirit of pride and progress. A bumper sticker from the era said it all: "Cerritos—The Freeway City—A Prestige Address—The Geographic Center of Southern California."

Top: The Cerritos City Council accepted a formal resolution from the California State Assembly on February 21, 1967, recognizing the city's name change from Dairy Valley to Cerritos. Accepting the resolution are from left, Council-members Jim Albers and Frank Leal, Mayor Pro Tem Louis Struik-man, Mayor Fred Troost, and Councilmember Tony Cordeiro.
Bottom: *California Governor Ronald Reagan (left) meets with Cerritos representatives in Sacramento on March 2, 1967, recognizing the city's name change. Pictured with Reagan are (left to right) Cerritos City Councilmembers Frank Leal, Tony Cordeiro, and Jim Albers, Mayor Fred Troost, Senator George Deukmejian, and Assemblyman Joe Gonsalves.*

Top Left: *The City of Cerritos officially makes its debut to motorists with the installation of new freeway signs. While the elevation hasn't changed (64), the population undoubtedly has.*

Top Right: *Miss Cerritos 1967–68, Nancy Albers, was the first to represent the newly named City of Cerritos. Selected by the Cerritos Chamber of Commerce based on poise, positive attitude, and professional appearance, Miss Cerritos represents the Chamber at luncheons, mixers, and grand openings.*

Left: *Known as the San Gabriel River Freeway, the 605 was built beginning in 1964. The 605's connection with the 105 is officially called the Joe A. Gonsalves Memorial Interchange in honor of one of Dairy Valley's native sons. A former mayor, Gonsalves served in the state legislature for twelve years.*

7

Forging Ahead through the 1970s

Homes, Sweet Homes

Thanks to the network of new and modern freeways, commuters were now zipping throughout Los Angeles and Orange counties in the 1970s, and Cerritos truly was the geographic center of Southern California. And thanks to a scramble by developers eager to build homes on the area's now-vacant cow pastures, Cerritos quickly became the building capital of Los Angeles County.

By 1971, exactly 3,367 building permits, valued at more than $90 million, were issued in Cerritos, representing 70 percent of the single family homes under construction in the county. Within the span of a few years, the city's population also exploded, from a count of 4,373 residents in 1968 to 37,748 residents counted during a special census in 1972. The area's assessed valuation boomed. While Dairy Valley's land had been worth $28.5 million in 1958, property in the new city of Cerritos was worth well over $124 million by 1973.

Addressing the City's "Blight"

Just as the dairy fields were slowly replaced by tidy, family homes, the dairymen on the city council were slowly replaced by engineers, salesmen, attorneys, and environmentalists. For the first time, in the early 1970s, there wasn't a single dairyman on the council. It was at this time the city began investigating a practice that promised to transform its remaining cow fields: redevelopment.

In the late 1940s, after World War II, suburban development began drawing residents and shoppers outside America's downtowns, leaving city centers—and often historic buildings—to deteriorate. To reverse this trend, the government passed legislation that allowed cities to replace slums and urban "blight" with prosperous new buildings. Cities could create "redevelopment agencies" to oversee improvements in specific "redevelopment zones." Revenue for improvements was generated by freezing taxes in the area and issuing bonds for the cost of new developments that, over time, would attract tenants and bring revenue and growth. Redevelopment agencies had the power to condemn buildings, relocate tenants, buy and resell land, make plans, and install streets and public facilities. Cities across the country used this process to rejuvenate entire neighborhoods and bring vital services to neglected areas.

While Cerritos didn't have slums or crumbling buildings, city leaders saw "blight" in the pasture lands that covered the city's west side. So on November 17, 1970, the Los Cerritos Redevelopment Agency was established, with authority over 820 acres bounded by the San Gabriel River on the west, Alondra Boulevard on the north, South Street on the south, and Studebaker Road, Eric Avenue, and Gridley Road on the east. With hopes for a prosperous future, the newly

Top: The sound of hammers and the smell of plywood pervaded Dairy Valley and Cerritos for much of the 1960s and into the 1970s. Here, a new batch of Cerritos homes takes shape along the freeway in April 1971.

Bottom: To protect residents from noise and dust, in 1972, Cerritos became the first city to require developers to build freeway buffer walls, which were said to reduce traffic noise to the level of a normal speaking voice. The city invested an additional $10 million in buffer walls throughout the 1980s.

Phase II of the Los Cerritos Center construction was completed in 1972, adding a wing from Ohrbach's (now Mervyns) to Sears. Today, the facility ranks as one of Southern California's leading shopping centers, with major department stores including Mervyns California, Macy's, Nordstrom, and Sears.

established Cerritos Redevelopment Agency (made up of the city council members) agreed to invest $30 million in the area, with visions for a large retail center and an innovative "auto mall."

Within a few short years, their plan began to bear fruit with the opening of Los Cerritos Center, a one-hundred-acre shopping complex built at Gridley Road and South Street by developer Ernest W. Hahn, Inc. The first phase opened in 1971 and the second in 1972. At last, residents rejoiced that they were able to shop locally at four major department stores—Sears, Robinsons, Broadway, and Ohrbach's—as well as 150 smaller specialty stores. A large Fedco department store was sited across the street.

Construction began on Los Cerritos Center in 1970, as a battalion of bulldozers, cranes, and crewmen arrived to build the new regional mall.

The city council and "Miss Cerritos" remained busy attending grand opening ceremonies and cutting ribbons—and at one time a long string of pearls—to open the new stores.

One of the area's first "shopping malls," Los Cerritos Center was completely covered, air-conditioned, and impeccably maintained. More important, the center accomplished exactly what it was supposed to, bringing thousands of dollars of sales tax revenue to the city. In fact, retail sales in Cerritos grew tenfold in just four years, topping $207 million in 1974. With this success, a *Los Angeles Times* report on redevelopment named Cerritos a prime example of what could be done with excellent planning and investment. Soon after, on May 7, 1975, the city set aside another 1,615 acres on the east side of town, to be called the Los Coyotes Redevelopment Zone.

Development Discord

But this success in Cerritos still failed to impress voters in neighboring Artesia. Hoping to streamline efforts to provide facilities and services, the city councils from the two towns proposed a merger in the early 1970s. The issue certainly touched a nerve, drawing three-fourths of Artesia's voters to the polls. The result: 1,140 "yes" votes and 1,362 "no" votes. With longstanding pride in their community, many Artesians balked at the idea of being absorbed by the young city next door. Others feared that their homes would be razed in favor of new development. Their fears were quelled by the resounding vote, and many of their homes stand today.

At the same time, local critters also fought to hold on to their territory. Housewives whose homes had been built near still-vacant fields were upset to find their backyards crawling with black widow spiders—a reminder that Cerritos hadn't been urban for very long. Local skunks, opossums, and foxes also dug in their heels, seeing no reason to leave, while meadowlarks and pheasants called to each other across open fields.

While the new homes didn't seem to affect the local wildlife, the city's strict zoning rules did ruffle a few feathers. In one legendary squabble, city leaders had a philosophical clash with the Chamber of Commerce, after which the city cut off the Chamber's $850 subsidy and even took back the office furniture. Longtime Chamber leader John Corcoran resigned for another post.

Local merchants also protested the city's strict sign ordinances, which received national attention when the city's new Toys "R" Us store was told the trademark "R" could not be

The Cerritos Chamber of Commerce

The Dairy Valley Chamber of Commerce was launched in 1963 by a group of local businessmen to "preserve the competitive enterprise system of business and to promote...growth and development." The group was formally incorporated in 1974 as the Cerritos Chamber of Commerce, and its original mission has endured.

Today, the Cerritos Chamber of Commerce is a member-driven, nonprofit association of business professionals and civic-minded residents committed to improving the business climate and quality of life in the Cerritos area. With more than four hundred members, the group promotes economic development and business retention, enhances government relations and community development, advances collaborative partnerships and alliances, and provides key resources for the community.

In the group's own words, the Chamber's goal is to promote and enhance the commercial, professional, economic, educational, cultural, and environmental well-being of Cerritos through a myriad of programs and activities, which include luncheon programs, networking events, educational programs, publications and timely information, and a membership that is dynamic and growing.

Through legislative advocacy, economic development campaigns, partnerships with local educational institutions, business development opportunities, and "member-only" benefits and services, the Cerritos Chamber of Commerce plays an integral role in sustaining existing businesses and helping them grow and succeed, as well as developing and attracting new businesses to help sustain our community.

The Cerritos Chamber of Commerce is located at 13259 South Street in Cerritos and can be reached at (562) 467-0800.

Taking the place of the strawberry fields at the corner of Bloomfield Avenue and 183rd Street, Cerritos Public Library was designed as a source of community pride, independent of the county library system.

reversed in their sign. After the uproar, the city council decided instead to reverse its opinion. Nevertheless, the star at Carl's Jr. could not be on the roof, city leaders declared, and the Big Boy statue at Bob's restaurant would have to stand demurely in the restaurant lobby. The Big Yellow House restaurant was instead painted a tasteful cream. The city no longer needed billboard revenue, so these large roadside signs quickly disappeared, as did any neon signs, flashing lights, banners, or whirligigs that detracted from the city's refined countenance.

Local contractor A. J. Padelford & Son handled the construction of Cerritos Public Library, using blueprints from architect Maurice Fleishman, AIA.

After a few legal tests, the state supreme court upheld the city's right to make zoning changes in local land use, and the county superior court gave its nod to the Cerritos sign ordinance. The rules still stand today.

Glorious Growth

Despite these bumps in the road, Cerritos continued to set its own course through the early '70s with a series of high-profile developments that would shape the enduring character of this new city.

First on the list was a new library. After a long debate over whether to rejoin the county library system and share a branch library with Artesia, Cerritos opted instead to build its own facility. A site was chosen at the corner of Bloomfield Avenue and 183rd Street, and a festive groundbreaking ceremony was held in June 1972, just after the strawberries had been harvested from the field. Fittingly, revelers feasted on a fifteen-foot-long strawberry shortcake.

The first building added to the city's Civic Center, the library was officially dedicated on October 13, 1973, with eighteen thousand square feet of space

and more than forty-five thousand volumes. The new facility also provided the latest technology, including 16-mm sound films and projectors, dozens of magazines on 16-mm microfilm cartridges, record players with headphones, coin-operated electric typewriters, and copy machines. The new library also had a large children's area, a theater, and a law library. With a nod to our area's most notable resident, former first lady Patricia Nixon, the new library was dedicated to the First Ladies of the Nation, both past and present. An active Friends of the Library group mobilized to support the library's programs and, three years later, Cerritos joined the Metropolitan Cooperative Library System, giving patrons access to more than three million items at twenty-six member libraries.

Seeing Green

At the same time, Cerritos continued to add to its collection of neighborhood parks. In the winter of 1971, seven parks were simultaneously being designed or built. City Park East (now Cerritos Park East) on 166th Street was the first large facility to be completed. The twenty-two-acre site featured more than 350 newly planted trees, plus three baseball diamonds, a multipurpose field, basketball, handball, and shuffleboard courts, a picnic area, and two playgrounds. An 8,600-square-foot community center was added later, including a multipurpose room, an arts and crafts room, a weight room, a game room, and a kitchen. The park quickly became the favored site for the city's Octoberfest and the annual Fourth of July "Let Freedom Ring" celebration, which featured all-day entertainment and an after-dark fireworks extravaganza.

Top: A. J. Padelford founded a local construction company in 1931, building barns and small homes. Today, his award-winning Cerritos-based company, A. J. Padelford & Son, Inc., boasts a seventy-year history and an extensive list of projects that includes the original Cerritos Library and much of the Cerritos Auto Square.

Bottom: State legislators George Deukmejian (second from left) and Joe Gonsalves (second from right) joined the Cerritos City Council in dedicating Cerritos Public Library on October 13, 1973. Unveiled along with the eighteen-thousand-square-foot brick building was a collection of forty-five thousand books.

While CPE was completed, sod was carefully laid at Brookhaven, Ecology, Friendship, Gridley, Jacob, Loma, Saddleback, Sunshine, and Westgate parks, providing Cerritos families with colorful play equipment, plenty of grass for running and games, and picnic facilities for sunny afternoons. The parks were added in strategic spots suggested by citizens' committees who hoped to provide green space within walking distance of every Cerritos home and at least an acre of parkland for every one hundred residents.

Soon after, Bettencourt Park, built over a former dump near Coyote Creek, received an environmental planning award from the California Park and Recreation Society. The park featured a steep slope of which the city of "little hills" was a bit deficient. Later, Reservoir Hill Park, at Gridley Road and 166th Street, provided an innovative cover for the city's twelve-million-gallon water storage

Dairy Valley's Own: First Lady Patricia Nixon

One of the area's most notable residents, former First Lady Patricia Nixon, was born on March 16, 1912, in Ely, Nevada, and quickly named Thelma Catherine Ryan by her mother. When her father came home past midnight after working in the mines, he dubbed his new daughter "St. Patrick's babe in the morn." From that moment on, she was to be known as "Pat."

Before young Pat was a year old, her family moved to a small farm in Dairy Valley, near the corner of today's South Street and Ely Avenue. When her mother died in 1925, Pat, now thirteen, assumed responsibility for running the household for her father and brothers. When her father became ill two years later, Pat cared for him until his death in 1930.

A graduate of Excelsior High School, Pat paid her way through Fullerton Junior College by working as a part-time janitor at a local bank. She later graduated cum laude from the University of Southern California with a teaching certificate. Her first job was teaching business education at Whittier Union High School for $1,800 a year, where she became a popular figure on campus.

After joining the Whittier Little Theater group, Pat starred with a young lawyer named Richard Nixon in a 1937 mystery drama. The drama turned into a love story, and the Nixons were married on June 21, 1940, and settled into a home in Whittier. While Mrs. Nixon continued

Former First Lady Patricia Nixon is shown in this official portrait courtesy of Richard Nixon Library & Birthplace.

teaching, Mr. Nixon continued his private law practice. Mr. Nixon's political career later took root, just as the Nixons celebrated the births of two daughters, Tricia and Julie. Mr. Nixon won a seat as a United States senator in 1950 and two years later became vice president of the United States under President Dwight D. Eisenhower.

Mrs. Nixon soon earned a reputation as a goodwill ambassador, joining her husband on trips to fifty-three countries. By 1968, Mr. Nixon decided to run for president, and his wife served as a significant force in his campaign.

As First Lady, Mrs. Nixon championed volunteerism, launched a literacy program, pushed for new parks in big cities, and traveled to more than eighty countries. She regularly toured schools, hospitals, orphanages, and homes for the

A bronze statue depicting former First Lady Pat Nixon was dedicated at the site of her childhood home on March 1, 1997. Crafted by East Coast artist Ivan Schwartz, it is one of the first life-size, full-body statues created in the image of a United States First Lady. Copyright Marcus Tate.

elderly. For her work in delivering supplies after a devastating earthquake, Peru awarded Mrs. Nixon the Grand Cross of the Order of the Sun, the oldest honor in the Americas.

At home, Mrs. Nixon promoted preservation of the White House, arranged tours for visually and hearing impaired visitors, and instituted after-hours candlelight tours of the building. She also paid respect to her hometown roots, attending a groundbreaking on September 5, 1969, of the Cerritos park that bears her name and making a rare public appearance to dedicate Patricia Nixon Elementary School in 1975. Her husband had resigned the presidency the year before. The couple later retired to the beaches of San Clemente. Mrs. Nixon died on June 22, 1993, in New Jersey and was buried on the grounds of the Nixon Library in Yorba Linda. In Cerritos, Mrs. Nixon's likeness stands in bronze near the site of her childhood home, surrounded by a bed of roses.

From the Richard Nixon Library and Birthplace On-Line, www.nixonfoundation.org/TheNixons/PatNixon.shtml.

City leaders eyed this vacant plot of land on 166th Street, next to a tract of newly built homes, as the perfect location for a large community park. City Park East (now Cerritos Park East) opened soon after in 1972.

The community center at City Park East featured striking brick arches, designed by architects from Weldon J. Fulton Associates. The center was upgraded in 1996 with a $2 million expansion and renovation, including a banquet hall that seats four hundred guests. Copyright Marcus Tate.

reservoir while adding another "little hill" to the city's collection.

By now, plans were also underway to transform another "hill" that had become a nuisance to neighbors in La Palma and Lakewood. The old fertilizer cooperative at the corner of Del Amo Boulevard and Bloomfield Avenue had become an informal dirt bike course for local daredevils, dubbed Motorcycle Park, and neighbors weren't happy about the buzz of the bikes or the lingering smell of manure. With help from the county, the property was transformed into the fifty-six-acre Cerritos Regional County Park, featuring a gymnasium, a fishing lake, a fifty-meter outdoor swimming pool, playing fields, tennis and basketball courts, picnic grounds, and bike paths. The land was purchased with $1.5 million in city funds matching a federal Housing and Urban Development grant and built using $6 million of county revenue bonds. The dedication gala on October 22, 1977, lasted all day long, with the buzz of dirt bikes replaced by music from the Artesia, Cerritos, and Gahr high school bands, and the aroma of cows replaced by the scent of sizzling hot dogs.

An 8.6-acre park—dubbed Parksite No. 15—completed in 1974 on Studebaker Road was another major accomplishment. Residents were given their choices for a name—Americana, Centennial, Independence, Justice, or Liberty—

citing the country's fast-approaching bicentennial celebration. Liberty Park had a special ring, voters decided, and the name stuck. The park's five-thousand-square-foot community center offered a meeting room, a weight room, an arts and crafts room, and a kitchen, while the spacious park provided a baseball diamond and playing fields, basketball, volleyball, handball, and tennis courts, and a wading pool for little ones. Smiling city leaders distributed miniature American flags to more than one thousand revelers at the park's December 14 dedication ceremony.

The following year, the city honored its most famous one-time resident by dedicating the Pat Nixon Home and Museum at 12364 South Street, the site of the former first lady's childhood home and her family's truck farm. The five-room house was restored and authentically decorated, set on four acres of rolling lawns at Pat Nixon Park.

As the country celebrated its two hundredth anniversary in 1976, Cerritos joined in with a parade, a Heritage Fair carnival, special excursions, and, soon after, the opening of the bicentennial-themed Heritage Park. The city had bought the fifteen-acre parcel at Bloomfield Avenue near 183rd Street from De Voss Dairy in 1973, including the De Voss home at 18600 Bloomfield Avenue that was soon converted to a youth center. Initial plans for the park were modest, but by its opening in the spring of 1977, the site had been transformed into every child's dream. It featured a three-acre Revolutionary War–themed adventure island complete with a New England–style village and covered bridge surrounded by a lagoon. Paul Revere on horseback joined actor Richard Dreyfuss, *Grizzly Adams* star Dan Haggerty and his bear, Ronald McDonald, Mickey Mouse, Donald Duck, and KNBC-TV personalities Kelly Lange and Paul Moyer in welcoming a crowd of revelers at the park's dedication.

Meanwhile, local golfers rejoiced with the 1977 opening of the new twenty-nine-acre, nine-hole executive golf course, dubbed Iron-Wood Nine, which lined the 605 Freeway. The $682,000 facility, funded by the city's redevelopment

Top: Now encompassing thirty-two acres, Cerritos Park East offers a spacious community center, baseball diamonds, basketball, handball, and tennis courts, colorful playgrounds, picnic shelters, and a refreshing spray pool for summer afternoons. Copyright Marcus Tate.
Bottom: *Renovated in 1996, the Cerritos Park East Community Center is a hub for city classes and activities, featuring dedicated rooms for games, arts and crafts, and dance and fitness classes. Its rooms, including the 6,758-square-foot California Room, can be reserved for weddings, special events, and meetings.*

As with other city parks, Brookhaven was carefully located within walking distance of nearby homes. The 2.5-acre park continues to attract neighborhood families, with colorful playground equipment, a basketball court, and picnic tables under the trees.

With the goal of creating an acre of parkland for every one hundred residents, city leaders were open to unusual locations. Reservoir Hill Park at Studebaker Road and 166th Street provided a grassy green cover for the city's twelve-million-gallon water reservoir, as well as a fun place for local kids to roll down a hill.

The city's park maintenance crews are on the job daily, making sure the city's collection of twenty-one parks are in prime shape for visitors. The five-acre Jacob Park offers lush lawns, shady picnic spots, playing fields, courts, and playground equipment. Copyright Marcus Tate.

Local daredevils race for glory at Cerritos' Motorcycle Park in 1974. Actually an old dusty field that once served as a fertilizer cooperative, the unofficial park attracted a daily contingent of BMX and motorbike enthusiasts until it was converted to Cerritos Regional County Park in 1977.

Clouds of balloons decorated the dedication gala at Cerritos Regional County Park on October 22, 1977. Thousands of residents turned out for a full day of festivities, food, and music.

Former first lady Pat Nixon's childhood home was completely restored, authentically decorated, and converted to a community museum in the early 1970s.

Cerritos leaders worked closely with the county of Los Angeles to develop the fifty-six-acre Cerritos Regional County Park, using county bond funds. County Supervisor James Hayes (left) joined Cerritos Mayor Pro Tem Barry Rabbitt (right) in welcoming revelers at the Cerritos Regional County Park's 1977 dedication.

The remains of the old De Voss Dairy are removed from the land at 18600 Bloomfield Avenue in December 1975, making way for the fifteen-acre Heritage Park. The De Voss family home was preserved and converted to a community center.

The ambitious plans for Heritage Park called for a three-acre play island complete with a New England–style village. Watched over by the new church steeple, bulldozers clear the way for a surrounding lake in September 1976.

agency, featured a three-hundred-yard lighted driving range, a Pro Shop, a starter's booth, and a restaurant, and it was open from sunrise to sunset. Even more innovative, the course was irrigated with water recycled by the adjacent Los Coyotes Water Reclamation Plant.

Later in the decade, the Cerritos Redevelopment Agency worked in cooperation with the ABC Unified School District to build the $2.5 million Hanford Rants Stadium at Gahr High School, including a five-thousand-seat stadium, an all-weather track, a football and soccer field, and a gymnasium expansion.

New Schools for New Students

Just as Cerritos grew, so did the ABC Unified School District. The administrative offices moved to a brand new complex at 166th Street and Norwalk Boulevard, and ten new schools were completed between 1969 and 1974. A new Carmenita Junior High campus replaced the old Carmenita

The twenty-nine-acre Cerritos Iron-Wood Nine Golf Course offers nine challenging holes open from dawn to dusk, plus a driving range, an on-site café, and lessons for players of all ages and abilities. Copyright Marcus Tate.

With discount greens fees for Cerritos residents, junior golfers, and seniors, Iron-Wood Nine Golf Course has become a favorite of local duffers. A lighted three-hundred-yard driving range is open into the evening hours for players who'd like to practice their swing. Copyright Marcus Tate.

Since Heritage Park's opening in 1977, generations of Cerritos children have crossed this covered bridge, walking back in time. The Revolutionary War–themed island mixes a gentle history lesson with plenty of space for active play.

Hanford Rants Stadium at Gahr High School, built in cooperation with the Cerritos Redevelopment Agency, is a favored facility for school sporting events, regional tournaments, homecoming games, graduations, and special assemblies.

Xerox is just one of dozens of national firms that have selected Cerritos Industrial Park as their regional headquarters. A Kosmont Cost of Doing Business Survey rated Cerritos "one of the most affordable and business-friendly cities in Southern California."

School, but the old building was retained for use by ABC Adult School. Work was also completed on a new continuation high school called El Dorado (now called Tracy), and Cerritos High School was completed in 1973 to serve students on the east side of town. Whitney Education Center on Shoemaker Avenue was dedicated in September 1976, the last school facility to be built by the district. At the same time, the Cerritos College campus expanded to cover 140 acres, serving nearly eleven thousand registered students.

Cerritos Industrial Park

While new schools and parks helped confirm Cerritos as one of the county's best communities for young families, it was also attracting its fair share of commercial firms. The Cerritos Industrial Park, bounded by Bloomfield Avenue, 166th Street, Carmenita Road, and the city limits, provided a perfect site for forward-thinking companies. It boasted modern buildings and spotless surroundings, not to mention a central location with easy access to three major freeways, rail lines, airports, and the ports of Long Beach and Los Angeles. Airstream Trailer, All American Nut Company, and TMCO Carburetor were among the first tenants,

joined soon after by Fashion Furniture and La Veche.

To preserve the city's character and minimize any effects on neighboring homes, city codes for the industrial center remained strict. There were to be no noxious uses, heavy manufacturing, or truck terminals. Noise, odors, glare, vibration, and exhausts were to be controlled, and storage, refuse, and maintenance areas had to be screened from public view. The industrial buildings were set back and softened with lawns, trees, and flowers, planted to provide a park-like atmosphere.

Rather than deterring tenants, these high standards helped attract world-class firms. Today, businesses within the 845-acre master-planned center provide thousands of jobs in light manufacturing and assembly of electronic and automotive parts, as well as countless other products. The park is also home to the city's largest employer, the United Parcel Service, and its staff of five thousand.

A New City Hall

While employees at the Cerritos Industrial Park were enjoying top-notch facilities, the city's 158-person staff had become used to a hodgepodge of temporary offices and trailers at the old city hall on Pioneer Boulevard. Council meetings were held in high school auditoriums across the city, the only venues big enough to accommodate an audience.

The situation changed dramatically on March 18, 1978, with the dedication of the new fifty-two-thousand-square-foot Cerritos City Hall. Located at 183rd Street and Bloomfield Avenue, adjacent to Cerritos Public Library, the three-story building featured an ultramodern style created by the same architect, Maurice H. Fleishman, AIA, who designed the library. The adjacent council chambers, equipped with state-of-the-art audiovisual equipment and stadium seating, could accommodate 165 people.

Top: The Cerritos Distribution Center II, part of the Cerritos Industrial Park, provides easy truck access for local firms while minimizing noise and other impacts on nearby residential neighborhoods. All totaled, the park offers 845 acres and 16.3 million square feet of industrial space housing hundreds of companies.

Bottom: The city selected the same architect who designed the Cerritos Public Library, Maurice H. Fleishman, AIA, to create the new Cerritos City Hall. Here, the modern fifty-two-thousand-square-foot, three-story structure begins to take shape in November 1976.

Solar collector panels located on Cerritos City Hall's roof harness energy from the sun to provide space heating and hot water throughout the building.

Congratulating Cerritos on opening the first solar-powered public building in the United States, Governor Jerry Brown was a featured speaker at City Hall's dedication ceremony on March 18, 1978. Governor Brown spoke on the importance of preserving natural resources and protecting the Earth.

Beside the new building were an open-air amphitheater, decorative fountains, a small park, lush landscaping, and a new concrete seating area. But the highlight was on the roof, where a one-of-a-kind solar energy system was installed. Using a $40,000 grant from the federal Energy Research and Development Administration, Cerritos City Hall became the first public building in the country to employ solar energy. Nearly 1,408 square feet of solar panels would collect roughly 320,500,000 BTU of heat per year, with the energy stored in two 1,500-gallon heat transfer tanks. The scientific marvel provided 57 percent of the building's space heating needs and 95 percent of energy needed for potable hot water, cutting natural gas use by 67 percent.

The timing was perfect. In the late 1970s, a gas shortage had focused Americans' attention on the need to conserve energy and protect our natural resources. Leading the way, public buildings across the country cut back on heating, lighting, and air conditioning. The new Cerritos City Hall served as a model, and nearly two thousand citizens joined representatives from the county, state, and federal governments to celebrate its opening. Mayor Robert Witt turned the podium over to Governor Jerry Brown, who delivered a speech on the benefits of solar technology.

A diagram of Cerritos City Hall's solar power system remains in the building's lobby to promote the benefits of solar energy. Rooftop collector panels are connected to a circulating water loop and heat pump system, providing most of the energy needed for space and hot water heating.

The city continued to delve into solar power through the 1970s, adding solar energy features at the new Corporate Yard built on Marquardt Avenue that was to house the city's maintenance crews and equipment. The city council voted to require subdivision builders to include solar collectors on half of the new homes they built, and a solar power system figured prominently in the design of a new "natatorium," or indoor swim center, planned on 166th Street.

Cerritos City Hall remains a visible part of the Civic Center skyline, much as it did at its 1978 opening. The open and accessible building welcomes visitors with friendly front-counter staff providing a range of city services.

Auto Square

The climate was also sunny on the west side of town that year, as plans were in the works for another innovation: the Cerritos Auto Mall. Defying the conventional wisdom that competing retailers shouldn't locate next door to one another, the city's original General Plan had called for a one-stop car shopping heaven. By 1977, the Cerritos Redevelopment Agency remained convinced that

As with most of the city's major developments, Cerritos Auto Square was once dairy land. This photo shows Studebaker Road in the foreground, between South and 183rd Streets. To create the auto mall, the city purchased land from Jake Knevelbaard Dairy and seven other property owners.

shoppers would flock to an "auto mall" that offered every car and truck imaginable. "We knew that Cerritos offered a unique blend of available land, a large market threshold, excellent location in relation to a large regional shopping center and freeway access," read early marketing brochures.

Leaders had zeroed in on a plot of about ninety acres along the San Gabriel River, within the redevelopment zone, that offered outstanding visibility and easy on- and off-ramps from the 605 Freeway. In 1979, the Redevelopment Agency started laying the groundwork for the new auto mall, purchasing land from Jake Knevelbaard Dairy and seven other property owners and making improvements to what would be its main stretch, Studebaker Road between 183rd and South streets. At the same time, the agency aggressively pursued potential tenants, luring them with the promise of low land costs, a great location, and a new fenced storage area for one thousand vehicles along the Southern California Edison power line right-of-way.

By October, five major auto dealers had joined local officials for a groundbreaking ceremony marking the start of construction of the $23 million project. Dixieland music played, and guests enjoyed an antique car show and refreshments under a 3,200-square-foot tent erected for the occasion. During Phase I, S&J Chevrolet, Moon Datsun, Cerritos Dodge, and Browning Oldsmobile joined Jim Snow Ford, which had set up shop a few years earlier near South Street. Others quickly followed, some drawn from neighboring communities who were chagrined at losing their sales tax revenue to a community they had once dismissed as a collection of cow pastures.

Cerritos Auto Square quickly became a regional destination after

Hoping to strike gold with the idea of a regional auto mall, Cerritos city leaders and representatives from five major auto dealers broke ground on the innovative project in 1980. The dignitaries are pictured at the future home of Browning Oldsmobile.

its official dedication on August 23, 1980, with rolling lawns and magnolia trees, an ornate gazebo with a large clock, turn of the century–style street fixtures and cobblestone intersections adding to its "New Orleans" atmosphere. Cerritos Auto Square, early brochures read, was to be "the business location for the 1980s and beyond!" Vacancies filled quickly.

Architects were kept busy sketching plans for a string of full-service dealerships with service bays. The buildings followed a New Orleans theme, with plenty of decorative wrought iron details. S&J Chevrolet was one of the Cerritos Auto Square's original tenants.

Unrivaled selection, spotless maintenance, and beautiful surroundings are just a few of the attractions that have drawn millions of car buyers to Cerritos Auto Square. Many of the dealerships, including Cerritos Mitsubishi, shown here, include the city's signature waterfalls, meandering sidewalks, and manicured landscaping.

Cerritos Auto Square filled in quickly, as this aerial photo of Studebaker Road shows. The new auto square boasted easy access from the 605 Freeway and close proximity to the already thriving Los Cerritos Center. Both factors helped to draw throngs of eager shoppers.

A **Decade** of **Growth:**
the **1980s**

8

Finishing Touches

By the 1980s, Cerritos could certainly be considered a thriving city. With a strong foundation firmly set in place, leaders could now turn their attention to finishing touches that would complete their suburban success story.

A new wing was added to Los Cerritos Center, featuring an upscale Nordstrom department store with a new row of specialty boutiques. "Restaurant Row" along 183rd Street just north of the center brought the number of local eateries to an impressive thirty-five (although fast-food drive-throughs were still outlawed).

Beautification efforts continued citywide. Street medians were planted with pine and eucalyptus trees, blooming daylilies, and agapanthus. Walls separating housing tracts from the city's major streets were covered with creeping fig and other vines that not only created vistas of green but also cleverly thwarted vandals. Parkways were lined with trees, shrubs, and flowers, and even commercial parking lots were required to have planted dividers. To help irrigate all of this greenery, work was now underway on a system that would bring recycled wastewater to parks, medians, and other green spaces. Wherever possible, utility lines were buried underground to preserve the city's beautiful vistas.

City Hall continued to expand its array of services and programs for residents and visitors, making Cerritos a much-desired address. Helping to safeguard the community, the Sheriff's Department developed crime intervention programs and organized Neighborhood Watch groups citywide. The city provided $1.2 million in funding for Fire Station #30, a traditional brick firehouse on Pioneer Boulevard that would become part of the county's Battalion 9. The station would house ladder and pumper trucks, plus a paramedic unit serving the western portion of Cerritos. Meanwhile, cleanup crews were quickly dispatched to erase any graffiti that appeared on city walls. The city also developed an appreciation for the special needs of its disabled residents, reworking curbs to make corners more convenient for wheelchairs and setting aside handicapped parking spaces at all public and commercial parking lots.

Diversity Rules

Just as the city's appearance was changing, so was the makeup of its residents. While Dutch, Portuguese, and Anglo names still lined the phone book, they were joined by names from many other nationalities. The U.S. Census in the late 1970s gave a snapshot of the city's 46,212 residents. Just over two-thirds were Caucasian, 5.2 percent were black, 10.2 percent were Asian, and 9.3 percent

Top: *Cerritos Mayor Alex Beanum (in car) and Mayor Pro Tem Don Knabe (right) congratulate restaurant manager Kelvin Chan on the April 1981 opening of Szechwan Chinese Cuisine in the city's new Restaurant Row. The string of eateries continues to tempt local diners with a range of international flavors.* **Bottom:** *A resident enjoys a stroll down a shady Cerritos thoroughfare. Winding sidewalks, beds of colorful flowers, shady trees, and vine-covered walls create a park-like atmosphere in every corner of the city. Copyright Marcus Tate.*

Backed by two fully outfitted fire trucks, Cerritos city leaders joined Los Angeles County Fire Department brass in January 1984 to celebrate the opening of Fire Station #30.

Since the city's incorporation in 1956, the Los Angeles County Sheriff's Department has continued to add to its list of services provided to the Cerritos community. Roy the German shepherd was a beloved member of the Lakewood Sheriff's Station's K-9 unit, dutifully serving Cerritos.

Cerritos Fire Station #30, located at 19030 Pioneer Boulevard, now serves as division and Battalion 9 headquarters for the Los Angeles County Fire Department. The fully stocked station is on call serving the Cerritos community twenty-four hours a day, seven days a week. Copyright Marcus Tate.

were Hispanic. These residents lived in 13,204 homes, and three-fourths of them owned their homes, which were valued at $25,000 to $70,000 or more. Just 4 percent of the wage earners worked in Cerritos, while another 71 percent commuted more than twenty miles to work. More than half of the city's residents had degrees or some college education, and they earned an average of $15,000 to $35,000 per year.

The 1977 city election brought to the city council new faces that reflected changing times and demographics. Diana S. Needham, a woman and an environmentalist, and Alex H. Beanum, an African American engineer, were elected, as was Frank Lee, who later resigned. Dr. Daniel K. Wong, a Chinese American doctor, was chosen to take his place during a special election. Councilmembers Dennis G. Bradshaw and Barry A. Rabbitt rounded out the group.

The *Los Angeles Times* fretted over Cerritos's growing ethnic diversity and the appearance of "white flight." But local residents knew the truth. Most families who moved from Cerritos were not "fleeing" but rather following job transfers or "moving up" to new luxury homes in Orange County. The *Times* also neglected to note that the city's non-Caucasian newcomers were often more affluent and more educated than the city's original homeowners. The newspaper changed its tune in 1984 with another spotlight on Cerritos, this time describing the city as "a suburban success: an experiment in urban design [that] resulted in a progressive, tax-rich city." Cerritos now ranked second after Bethesda, Maryland, as the wealthiest city of its size in the nation. The median income was now $31,813, and the median home cost was $120,000.

An Olympic Fete

Soon, the city's qualities would become known to thousands of Southland visitors with the arrival of the 1984 Olympic Games in Los Angeles. The "Cerritos Natatorium" on 166th Street was finished just in time, in 1982, to host practice sessions for several international synchronized swim teams who would compete in the Olympics for the very first time. Adjacent to Cerritos Park East, the state-of-the-art facility was situated on ten acres, which were purchased from the ABC Unified School District. It featured an enclosed fifty-meter pool with dressing rooms, a snack bar, a press box area, and seating capacity for fourteen hundred spectators. Even more novel were the building's rooftop

Just as farm families from all nationalities joined together at Dairy Valley's schools, churches, and downtown stores, new generations of Cerritos children have continued and enriched this diversity. Here, smiling summer campers get ready for their next fun activity.

Construction began on the Cerritos Olympic Swim Center in 1982, across the driveway from the Cerritos Park East community center. This aerial photo shows an early view of the park, before its canopy of trees filled in.

Plasterers smooth the shallow end of the Swim Center's Olympic-sized pool in March 1982, getting it ready for swimmers.

retractable skylights, illumination, cooling louvers, and solar panel system that helped to heat the pool water and showers year-round. (A Fitness Center added the following decade provided a multimax station, treadmills, stair climbers, lifecycles, and other fitness equipment for patrons' use.)

Olympic excitement spread across town, with colorful banners decorating the Cerritos Civic Center and major thoroughfares. Several Cerritos residents took part in the fifteen-thousand-kilometer, eighty-two-day relay that carried the Olympic torch across the country, from the United Nations Plaza in New York through thirty-three states to the Los Angeles Coliseum. Traffic was cleared from the Artesia Freeway (CA-91) for bike races, and local residents gathered to watch. Buses from Cerritos College transported sports fans to the Coliseum and other Olympic venues throughout Southern California. Although a boycott by the Soviet Union affected certain sports, more than 140 nations and nearly seven thousand athletes took part in 221 events.

Immediately after opening in 1982, the Cerritos Olympic Swim Center made a name for itself as a premier facility, complete with a fifty-meter heated pool, dressing rooms, a snack bar, a press box area, and seating for fourteen hundred spectators. Copyright Marcus Tate.

The Cerritos Olympic Swim Center now hosts hundreds of swim classes, recreational swim sessions, special events, and competitions each year, including popular synchronized swim meets. Copyright Marcus Tate.

Located directly across from the Cerritos Civic Center and visible from the 91 Freeway, this 125-acre field was one of the last remnants of the city's dairy days well into the 1980s. It was dubbed "Area Development Plan 2," otherwise known as "the Golden Triangle."

Towering palm trees, expanses of yellow daisies, and a rocky lagoon with waterfalls and fountains alerted motorists along the 91 Freeway that something special awaited in Cerritos. Improvements to the Shoemaker Avenue exit were the first signs of good things to come at Cerritos Towne Center. Copyright Marcus Tate.

"The Golden Triangle"

As competitors from around the globe vied for the gold that year, Cerritos leaders also hoped to strike gold in a dusty remnant of the city's past. An expansive 125-acre field bounded by the Artesia Freeway, Bloomfield Avenue, and 183rd Street remained as the last large undeveloped area in the community, and because of its obvious potential, local newspapers came to refer to it as "the Golden Triangle." The Los Coyotes Redevelopment Agency, however, took to calling the land "Area Development Plan 2," or ADP 2 for short, and began sketching out visions for its future.

By the early '80s, everyone seemed to have an opinion for the land's fate. Housing was out, most agreed, because whatever was built would need to generate tax revenue. A new golf course was nixed for the same reason. In 1970, a proposal was floated for a one-of-a-kind donut-shaped shopping center, but the idea was sunk by its proximity to Los Cerritos Center. By 1971, another proposal was on the table to build a Polynesian cultural center that would feature an artificial ocean with six islands and a volcano that would erupt nightly. The developers promised the volcano would be pollution controlled, but that wasn't enough to prevent eruptions from neighboring homeowners.

The most popular idea, backed by extensive market research, was to combine a public facility, such as a community theater or convention center, with a hotel and several office and commercial buildings. The city quickly went to work. Just as bulldozers began to clear the site, Cerritos aggressively pursued top-notch occupants and developers, tapping the talents of Transpacific Development Company to complete the multiphased project. Norwalk, Downey, and several other communities were either planning or building new hotels at the same time, so competition was fierce.

To set their project apart and lure motorists from the 91 Freeway, the redevelopment agency invested $8.6 million on an elaborate freeway overpass and access routes on Shoemaker Road, plus improvements along Bloomfield Avenue and 183rd Street. Like all of the city's previous developments, the property was extensively landscaped, with rambling sidewalks, a naturalistic stream with waterfalls and boulders, rolling lawns, and trees adding to the city's park-like ambiance.

While ADP 2 was by far the city's biggest project, a number of other large buildings were also in the works across town. Five new restaurants were added to Restaurant Row, including an eighteenth century–style British pub called Clinker Dagger, prompting the Chamber of Commerce to print a local dining guide of fifty eateries. Krausz Corporation finished the Cerritos Corporate Tower, filling the last site at Best Plaza, a center named for the two-story Best Products department store that served as its anchor. A branch post office was dedicated at Carmenita Road

Innovation in Irrigation

Some of the city's ingenuity can be found underground. Cerritos was one of the first cities in California to put recycled water into use, saving millions of gallons of drinking water every year.

The idea first took hold in the late 1970s with the opening of Cerritos Iron-Wood Nine Golf Course. In the midst of a statewide water shortage, city leaders noted that more than twenty million gallons of treated wastewater from the Los Coyotes Water Reclamation Plant were being dumped into

The city's recycled water is purchased from the Los Coyotes Water Reclamation Plant, which is operated by the Los Angeles County Sanitation District. The wastewater originates from industries, businesses, and homes, and is treated through a three-stage process by the Sanitation District before being used for irrigation.

the San Gabriel River daily. To stop the waste, the city agreed to purchase some of the treated water to irrigate the new golf course next door.

The project worked so well that, by the early 1980s, the city council had authorized the construction of an intricate system that would transport four thousand acre-feet of recycled water annually to parks, parkways, decorative fountains, and street medians citywide. The system was later expanded to provide recycled water, at half the price of drinking water, for the irrigation of schools, Cerritos College, freeway landscaping, the lawn and lakes at Cerritos Regional County Park, a cemetery, and other landscaped areas citywide. Much of the construction was covered by a $4.5 million grant from the State Water Resources Control Board to encourage water recycling.

Cerritos College is one of the many beneficiaries of the city's recycled water system, which helps to keep campus lawns green and flowers blooming. Photo courtesy of the Cerritos College Office of Public Affairs.

All totaled, the system now irrigates more than two hundred acres of city-owned property and conserves more than 815 million gallons of drinking water every year—a boon in our naturally dry region.

and 183rd Street, relieving crowds at the Artesia Post Office on the west side of town. By 1986, the city's land was 95 percent developed, with an assessed value of $2 billion. *South Coast Business* magazine featured Cerritos in its July issue, marveling that more than two thousand businesses were now located in this thriving burg. The city budget had topped $60.9 million, with $11.9 million collected as retail sales tax revenue.

The Library Expands

With smart planning and a thriving business climate, Cerritos had become one of the most financially stable communities in the county. And this stability allowed for the very best facilities and services for the city's fifty-five thousand residents.

An example was Cerritos Public Library. In 1986, the city embarked on a $6.1 million remodel of the thirteen-year-old building that would add twenty thousand square feet of badly needed space. The children's area was to be tripled to seven thousand square feet, including creative areas dedicated to arts and crafts, a sweeping mural of a fairy-tale castle, and a saltwater aquarium swimming with colorful species. The theater, which had become makeshift office and storage space, would again

Top: The City of Cerritos provided the funding for construction of the new U.S. Post Office at Carmenita Road and 183rd Street. The facility is open Monday through Friday from 7:30 a.m. to 4:30 p.m.
Bottom: Bulldozers tear down portions of the Cerritos Public Library in summer 1985 in preparation for a major expansion.

be used for public programs and performances. A large community room with dividers and kitchen facilities was made available for meetings and receptions, and a new wing included a large reference area, study space, and lounge seating. Visitors would be greeted with bright, open interiors with furnishings of polished brass, red oak cabinetry, etched glass dividers, and dark green marble counters. Not only did the project earn rave reviews from patrons, the expansion eventually won a national award of excellence, the top award given by the American Institute of Architecture and the American Library Association.

The building was undoubtedly well used. While just 20 percent of Americans regularly visit their local public library, the percentage in Cerritos topped 65 percent, with avid patrons borrowing nearly half a million books and other items every year. Statistics showed that the expansion had resulted in a 40 percent growth in the number of patrons and a 33 percent boost in the circulation of materials—money well spent, city leaders agreed.

Towering windows, open interiors, and beautiful furnishings and details helped earn Cerritos Public Library's 1986 expansion a national award of excellence from the American Institute of Architecture and the American Library Association. Copyright Marcus Tate.

A fanciful mural that swept across the Cerritos Public Library's new children's area helped stir imaginations and captivate young readers. Here, children's librarians Diane Wheatley (left) and Hedy Harrison (right) share a tale with three young charges. Copyright Marcus Tate.

The $6.1 million remodel of Cerritos Public Library in 1986 added twenty thousand square feet of space, including a spacious children's area, a public theater, a community room, and a new wing with a reference collection, study space, and lounge seating.

CERRITOS AIR DISASTER

THE TOLL 67 die as Aeromexico jet, small plane collide; as many as 10 killed on ground

By Richard Nordwind
Herald staff writer

An Aeromexico DC-9 jetliner flying into Los Angeles collided in midair with a small plane over Cerritos yesterday, then nosedived into a residential neighborhood, igniting homes and scattering bodies in its path.

The crash killed all 67 people aboard the two planes and as many as 10 people on the ground. It was the worst air disaster in Los Angeles County history.

Sixteen homes were destroyed or damaged by the flaming wreckage of the fuselage, trapping residents inside, the Los Angeles County Fire Department said.

With a burst of orange flames and a billow of black smoke, the plummeting jetliner, its tail knocked off, exploded into a tract of modest stucco homes.

The impact hurled passengers into walls, showered the neighborhood with jet parts, luggage and shredded bodies and sent a river of blood flowing down the streets.

The Aeromexico jet, arriving from Mexico, was on final approach to Los Angeles International Airport at 11:56 a.m. when a Piper Archer 2 single-engine plane smashed into the rear of the DC-9, sending the fuselage spiraling to the ground.

Aeromexico said 64 people — 58 passengers and six crew — were aboard the flight. The small plane, en route from Torrance to Big Bear, carried three people, the National Transportation Safety Board said.

Radar reports show the planes collided at an altitude between 6,200 to 7,000 feet, said Gary Mucho, the NTSB chief in Los Angeles. The DC-9 was flying west on a gradual descent into LAX, while the Piper was heading northeast.

Mucho said it was not known which plane hit the other. The crash occurred above Cerritos, about 36 miles southeast of Los Angeles near the Orange County line.

The DC-9 crashed into homes on Holmes Avenue and Ashworth Place near the Carmenita Road off-ramp of the Artesia Freeway. The Piper, the top of its cockpit sliced off, came down a half mile away in a ball field behind Cerritos Elementary. *Disaster/A-11*

PATH OF DEATH: After colliding with light plane, Aeromexico DC-9 hit ground at Ashworth Avenue, top right, sending debris through homes to Carmenita Road, left.

Circulation: 1,103,656 Daily / 1,368,105 Sunday   Monday, September 1, 1986   CC¼/ 82 Pages Copyright 1986/The Times Mirror Company   Daily 25¢

70 Die as Planes Collide in Air
Wreckage Plunges Into Cerritos, Burning 16 Homes

Covered human remains and debris at the crash site in Cerritos and, below, the falling Aeromexico jetliner after the collision.

Mexican Jetliner, Small Craft Intersect on Approach to L.A.

By TED THACKREY JR., *Times Staff Writer*

At least 70 people were killed, nine others were injured and 16 houses were set ablaze Sunday when a single-engine light airplane and an Aeromexico DC-9 jetliner collided in flight, crashing to earth in Cerritos and hurling flaming wreckage across a wide area.

The crash occurred at 11:56 a.m., and authorities identified the downed airliner as Aeromexico Flight 498, which was about to land at Los Angeles International Airport after a flight from Mexico City with stops in Guadalajara, Loreto and Tijuana.

Its main passenger cabin crashed upside down and exploded in a residential neighborhood near the corner of Carmenita Road and 183rd Street in Cerritos, damaging homes on Holmes Avenue, Reva Circle and Ashworth Place.

Eyewitnesses' Accounts

The cause of the disaster was not immediately determined, but eyewitnesses said they saw the smaller airplane crash into the tail section of the jetliner.

Airline spokesman Guy Areiola said 58 passengers and six crew members were aboard the DC-9 when it went down 20 miles east of the airport. Three people were reported to have been on board the smaller airplane, which crashed in an empty school yard about two blocks from the wreckage of the airliner.

"We are not aware of any survivors [from the two airplanes]," Los Angeles County Sheriff's Deputy Drew Baxey said.

Three more people were killed when their house at 13426 Ashworth Place was struck by blazing debris and immediately burst into flames, authorities said. No other ground fatalities could be confirmed, but firefighters said seven people were still missing hours after the crash.

Buena Park Police Officer Phil Martinez said he was on patrol when he saw the jetliner fall to earth—and explode on impact.

"I thought it was a balloon coming down," he said. "Then it hit and erupted in yellow and orange fire and smoke. Then I saw a smaller piece—I think it was the tail—coming down, and I knew it was a real disaster."

Timothy O'Brien, who lives in nearby La Palma, said. "The jet was upside down when it went in. I was coming home from the store and I had a clear view of the whole

The small plane in collision may have strayed into L.A. airport's approach path. Page 3. Additional crash stories and photos on Pages 3, 4, 5 and 20.

thing—the last part of it, anyway—and the big plane, the airliner, was upside down and didn't have a tail when it hit those houses and plowed into the ground and came apart."

At least three eyewitnesses said they saw the smaller airplane crash into the tail section of the jetliner, and in Mexico City an Aeromexico spokesman said agents from his company had found eyewitnesses who told them much the same story.

Aeromexico regional manager Rodolfo Casperino said his company's jetliner was proceeding at its *Please see PLANES, Page 4*

Local newspapers, including the Los Angeles Times *and the* Los Angeles Herald Examiner, *provided extended coverage of the 1986 Cerritos air disaster.*

Disaster Hits Home

True, Cerritos had become known for its planning, stability, and outstanding services. But nothing could have prepared the community for the events of Labor Day Weekend 1986. The city's enduring optimism took a tremendous hit on the morning of Sunday, August 31, when a small plane—a Piper Cherokee Archer II—collided midair with an Aeromexico DC-9 directly over the city, delivering unthinkable tragedy.

Within seconds, the Piper Cherokee fell to the unoccupied playground at Cerritos Elementary School on 183rd Street, narrowly missing the congregation filing out of Calvary Lutheran Church across the street after morning services. The enormous DC-9 plowed into a neighborhood just east of Carmenita Road and exploded, destroying eleven homes and damaging seven others on Ashworth Place, Holmes Avenue, and Reva Street. Fifteen Cerritos residents and visitors, all sixty-four passengers and crewmembers from the DC-9, and three people aboard the smaller plane were killed—a total of eighty-two lives lost.

Emergency crews from the Los Angeles County Fire and Sheriff's departments, as well as teams from Buena Park, La Palma, and Santa Fe Springs, responded immediately. City employees, the American Red Cross, community volunteers, and personnel from public service agencies from throughout the region, all hoping to help, quickly joined them. The area was closed off for what seemed an eternity as the wreckage was carefully examined and methodically hauled away.

A local Community Response Team joined forces with the Los Angeles County Department of Social Services to coordinate counseling programs and other necessities. A Cerritos Disaster Assistance Fund was established to provide help to residents of the crash area. More than twelve hundred people attended a memorial service conducted at Cerritos College by the Cerritos Ecumenical Council, and a booklet and program for dealing with trauma was offered to ABCUSD teachers so they would be prepared to help children when school opened the following week.

National newspapers, magazines, and radio and television programs covered the tragedy as attention was focused on the international problem of coordinating air traffic near busy airports. At City Hall, calls of concern were received from supporters around the world.

With teamwork and assistance from valued friends, the community slowly began its recovery later that fall. Families began to rebuild and repair their homes, fundraisers were held to aid disaster victims, "tourists" began to disappear, and eventually the crowds of media filed away to cover new stories. Investigations by the Federal Aviation Administration and National Transportation Safety Board drew on for months, attempting to pinpoint the cause of the accident and prevent future tragedies. The collision would eventually be blamed on "failure of the air traffic control system" and outdated equipment at the radar control center. This tragedy became known as the Cerritos Air Disaster and resulted in implementation of safer procedures for airport approaches and departures.

Staying Busy

With this tragic chapter in the city's history finally closed, in the following years the community slowly regained its sense of optimism, and work resumed on a series of noteworthy projects.

By the late 1980s, "the Golden Triangle" had been transformed into the Cerritos Towne Center, and its "gold" began to gleam. A plan had taken shape that called for hotel, office, commercial, and cultural amenities, with more than a million square feet of leasable space in twenty-three buildings. Leaders projected that, over its first fifty years, the $225 million center would generate $585 million in revenue for the city and provide forty-five hundred jobs. The national accounts division of Automatic Data Processing (ADP) moved into its new regional headquarters, becoming the first occupants of the first seven-story office building completed.

An Expert in Growth: Gaylord Knapp

At the helm during the city's prime development years was a man named Gaylord Knapp. Hired as the city's director of environmental affairs in 1973, Knapp was promoted to city manager just nine months later, carrying out the City Council's direction and shaping this growing city over the next eighteen years.

During his years in Cerritos, Knapp was actively involved in the Community Redevelopment Association of California, the Southern California Joint Powers Insurance Authority, the Southeast Los Angeles County Municipal Management Group, the International City Managers Association, and the American Planning Association. He left Cerritos in 1991 and was hired to lead the new City of Lake Forest in Orange County.

The Sheraton Cerritos Hotel was one of the first additions to the 125-acre Cerritos Towne Center. With its convenient location and luxurious amenities, the Sheraton frequently hosts performers from the Cerritos Center for the Performing Arts as well as vacationers and business travelers. Its ballroom is booked with community events. Copyright Marcus Tate.

Soon after, Transpacific Development Company finished work on the Sheraton Cerritos Hotel, and the facility opened its doors to great pomp and circumstance. A grand reception was held, treating more than six hundred community leaders to a tour with refreshments prepared by the hotel's world-class chefs. The guests walked wide-eyed through twenty-one beautifully appointed suites, ten conference rooms, the banquet room, and the full-service restaurant, also peeking inside models of the hotel's 203 private rooms. While the Towne Center's office buildings were starkly simple, with dark red granite façades, the hotel stood out with its light granite lower floors and expanses of dark blue glass. The round, ten-story central tower was flanked by two eight-story wings, sweeping at angles from each side. In front of the formal entrance remains a one-of-a-kind fountain. Water pours from the center of a large zinnia-shaped sculpture, gushing upward then flowing down and over the layered concrete "petals."

At the same time, farther north, seven buildings were finished at the Cerritos Corporate Center, on the last large parcel available in the industrial park. The last of the city's dairies was also demolished, a mint-green structure at Shoemaker Avenue and South Street that still boasted a sign that read "John Barcelos—Producer of Challenge Fresher Milk" ten years after it had closed. The dairy was replaced by thirty-eight new homes. Lincoln Station was completed on South Street, featuring a new Sportmart, shops, and restaurants.

Work was also underway on a unique telecommunications system. Since the city's early days, Cerritos had required all utilities to be buried underground, so it took several years to find a company willing to take on the expense of providing cable TV service. But in a joint venture, GTE of California and Apollo Cablevision installed a new system, burying 170 miles worth of coaxial cable under city streets. An experimental fiber-optic network was also installed in the northeast section of the city to test sophisticated video, voice, and data services—forerunners of systems that would be extended nationwide. Cerritos had been selected because of its "progressive orientation and desire to acquire the most advanced system possible."

The Cerritos Redevelopment Agency also worked to expand the now-thriving Cerritos Auto Square, purchasing an 8.5-acre site on the northwest corner of Studebaker Road

Shortly after the opening of the Sheraton Cerritos Hotel, construction began on several striking high-rise buildings, which filled in the Cerritos Towne Center's skyline. Today, dozens of companies and their employees enjoy the center's convenient location, beautiful surroundings, and close proximity to shops and restaurants.

The very last available parcel at the Cerritos Industrial Park was filled in the late 1980s by seven eye-catching buildings at Cerritos Corporate Center.

Workmen tear down a house and store marking Cerritos' last dairy farm, the John Barcelos Dairy, in April 1989.

Manuel Muñoz, a Cerritos resident since 1967, marvels at the changes taking place at the Cerritos Towne Center site. He and his son, Sigifredo Muñoz, spent an afternoon in 1989 capturing photos of the evolving landscape. Photo courtesy of the Muñoz family.

Opened in the late 1980s, Lincoln Station on South Street is one of the city's most successful shopping centers, featuring a convenient mix of stores, restaurants, banks, doctors' offices, real estate firms, and beauty salons, plus Blockbuster Video and Sportmart. Copyright Marcus Tate.

and 183rd Street that had once served as a turkey ranch and, later, a General Telephone Company service yard. The agency invested $1.2 million in improvements, including road enhancements, landscaped medians and parkways, rocky waterfalls, and decorative streetlights, laying the foundation for new Moothart Chrysler-Plymouth and Victory Pontiac-GMC dealerships. A few years later, a Saturn dealership was added, bringing the grand total of dealer franchises to twenty-two. Today, the Cerritos Auto Square covers 104 acres with twenty-six dealer points and more than four thousand spaces of off-site parking.

Liberty Park Expands

Just south of the Cerritos Auto Square, Liberty Park was enjoying an expansion of its own. With two years of construction and a $2.7 million budget, the popular park was enlarged to cover thirty-four acres tucked between the San Gabriel River and Studebaker Road, south of South Street. The new-and-improved park now included "Camp Liberty," a much-needed enclosed group picnic area, complete with barbecues, a stage, and a separate restroom facility, that provided a perfect spot for day camp activities, large celebrations, and overnight camping trips for the city's youth groups. A nearby amphitheater with grass seating for three hundred guests provided a breezy site for summer

Cerritos Pontiac Buick GMC was added to the northeast corner of Studebaker Road and 183rd Street, offering an array of new and pre-owned cars, trucks, and sport utility vehicles. As with most of the Cerritos Auto Square dealers, the dealership also offers a "virtual showroom" at www.cerritosgm.com.

Liberty Park was off-limits for a few months as heavy equipment was used to renovate its well-used community center and other park features in 1988. Soon after, Liberty received the Special Award of Excellence as the Best Community Park in the state from the California Park and Recreation Society.

concerts, casual performances, and youth sports awards programs. Local athletes enjoyed a new field and jogging track, four more lighted tennis courts, two lighted basketball courts, a Frisbee golf course, and four new indoor racquetball courts.

More than sixteen hundred residents celebrated the park's grand opening on January 7, 1989. And later that year, during a statewide awards program sponsored by the California Park and Recreation Society and ARCO, Liberty Park was presented with the Special Award of Excellence as the Best Community Park in the state, citing its "outstanding and unique achievements in park and recreational facility design and development."

Across town, another big crowd turned out the following year to celebrate the opening of the Cerritos Sports Complex. More than twenty-seven hundred revelers arrived for hot dogs, entertainment, and a peek at the luxurious new grounds during its dedication ceremony on February 3, 1990. Built on twenty-six acres chiseled from the Cerritos Regional County Park, the

The enclosed and sheltered Camp Liberty provided much-needed space for group picnics, special events and concerts, overnight camping trips, family reunions, and birthday parties. The fully equipped shelter is available for rental at nominal rates to Cerritos residents. Copyright Marcus Tate.

$4.9 million facility was designed to provide ample space for the city's organized sports teams, accommodating players of "all ages at all levels of play." The list of amenities was enough to make sports fans cheer, including three manicured softball fields, a combination baseball/softball field, a regulation baseball field, six fields for soccer or football, a sports office, and a concession stand with outdoor seating. The facility also boasted state-of-the-art lighting, an electric scoreboard and public address system for each field, aluminum stadium seating, and a stage for presentations.

Tennis courts are just the beginning of Liberty Park's offerings for local athletes. The park also offers a cushioned jogging track, a sand volleyball court, a Frisbee golf course, and lighted playing courts and fields.

After its construction, the twenty-six-acre Cerritos Sports Complex became the headquarters for local sports teams of all ages. The manicured facility provides ample space for concurrent softball, baseball, soccer, and football games, with comfortable seating and a concession stand for sports fans. Copyright Marcus Tate.

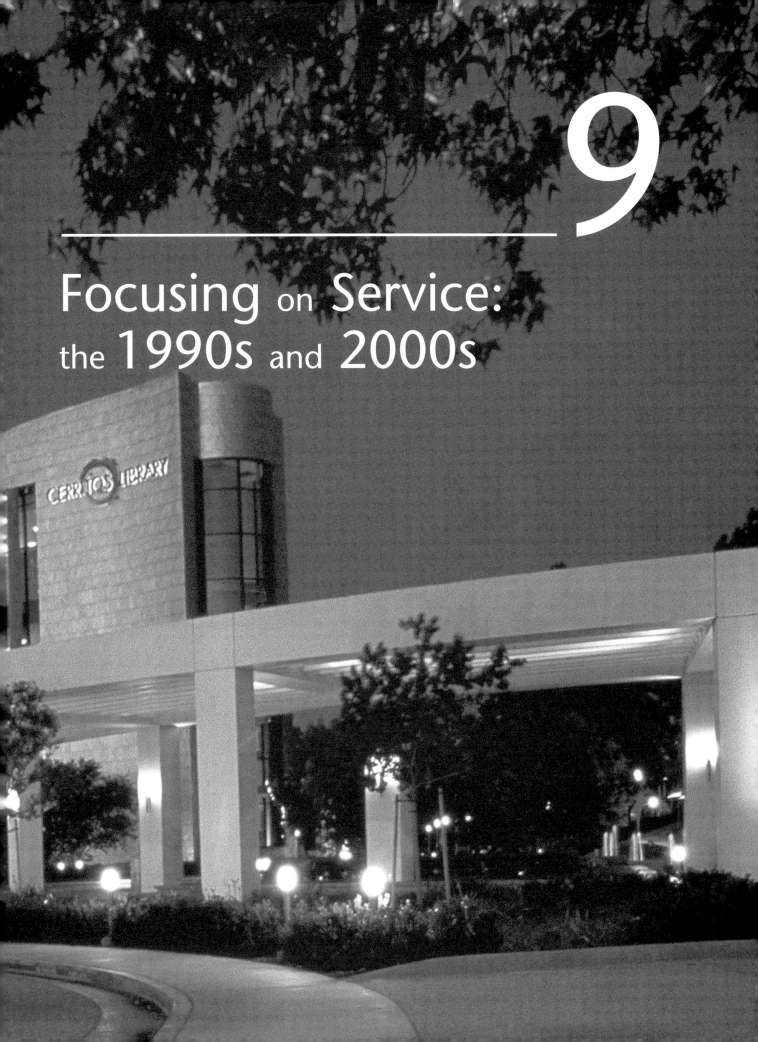

9

Focusing on Service: the 1990s and 2000s

*A*fter two decades of growth, by the early 1990s, the City was ready to build on the momentum of its accomplishments and further improve services offered to residents. With new priorities placed on superior maintenance and outstanding service, in 1991, the city council named longtime veteran Art Gallucci as city manager.

A father of five, Gallucci was first hired by the City in 1971. He quickly moved up to head the Human Affairs Department, starting in 1973, before being named assistant city manager in 1981. This lifelong public servant, the council felt, shared their love for Cerritos and would lead the community well into the next decades.

With beautiful flowers, tidy yards, well-kept paint, and decorative details, homeowners have helped make Cerritos a truly beautiful community. One hundred select property owners are honored each year at the Cerritos City Wide Pride banquet, recognizing outstanding home maintenance. Copyright Marcus Tate.

City Wide Pride

One of the first orders of business was to formalize the city's on-going beautification efforts. Since the 1950s and 1960s, the City and Chamber of Commerce had sponsored "Fix Up, Clean Up" campaigns to inspire owners to revitalize their properties and clear out debris left over from the city's dairy days. Each year, residents and business owners alike proudly pitched in to help restore the city's gleam.

To honor these efforts and to inspire more property owners to take part, the city council, consisting of Paul W. Bowlen, John F. Crawley, Ann Joynt, Sherman Kappe, and Daniel K. Wong, directed the Cerritos Property Preservation Commission to create the "City Wide Pride" program in January 1992. In what has become an annual spring cleaning, homeowners across the city were encouraged to sop up driveway oil stains, move old vehicles out of sight, plant new flowers, fix broken fences, polish windows, and touch up paint, with the aim of making Cerritos one of the best-looking cities in Southern California. Residents were also urged to nominate outstanding homes and businesses for a City Wide Pride Award.

By the program's first year, the homes that had been built during the city's boom were now reaching the fifteen- to twenty-five-year marks, and hundreds of owners were considering new roofs, room additions, landscaping, and other

The Edwards Stadium 10 Cinemas at the Cerritos Towne Center was named one of the most profitable locations in the Edwards chain. Nearby eateries are bustling at lunchtime, serving shoppers and employees from the Towne Center's high rises. Copyright Marcus Tate.

improvements. During City Wide Pride, the city took the opportunity to educate residents about home improvement rules and to tactfully spread the word about favored paint colors. While home builders had been required to stick to the "earth tone" palette popular in the '70s—shades of brown and beige, mossy green and avocado—color fashions had changed, and dozens of Cerritos homes were receiving new coats of paint. Hoping to keep the city's quiet neighborhoods free of any psychedelic designs or bubblegum-pink two-stories, city planners asked that homeowners bring their paint chips to City Hall for approval before opening any cans.

During its first year, the City Wide Pride program attracted 350 nominations, and the owners of eighty-one homes and ten businesses were honored at an April banquet at the Sheraton Cerritos Hotel. Dedicated volunteers judged the properties. It was quickly decided that City Wide Pride should be an annual event.

Cerritos Towne Center was home to one of the first Wal-Marts in the Los Angeles area. The center's mix of popular discount stores and restaurants struck a chord with local shoppers. A new Trader Joe's grocery store and Kohl's department store have added to the center's success. Copyright Marcus Tate.

Residents were eager to peek behind the fencing as construction began on the new Cerritos Community Arts Center in 1988. Its unusual shape piqued the interest of passersby.

Careful Financial Planning Benefits the City

While nearby communities struggled with economic challenges in the early '90s, Cerritos fought to protect the financial security it had worked so hard to achieve. Strapped for cash, neighboring cities floated the idea of distributing sales tax revenue regionally, which would have pulled millions from Cerritos's budget.

While the plan was scrapped and Cerritos was able to hold on to its revenue, city sales tax proceeds still fell by more than $3 million by 1992, and the redevelopment agency lost $2.8 million. The City survived the recession with modest budget cuts, new priorities, and delays on some projects. Nevertheless, Cerritos Public Library remained one of the only libraries to stay open seven days a week. Students, readers, and researchers drove from miles around, and standing-room-only was normal on evenings and weekends. The City's dedication to prudent financial planning and careful use of resources allowed the community to continue to enjoy a high level of services.

120

Meanwhile, despite budget challenges, ABC Unified School District was praised consistently for excellence. Test scores were among the highest in the state, and the district was revered for its outstanding bilingual education program. The district also offered a menu of extracurricular programs, including Model United Nations, school music programs, and sports, ranging from the usual football, baseball, and basketball to water polo, volleyball, and soccer. All of the district's high schools offered college prep and advanced placement classes, and with its high test scores, academic decathlons, and prestigious college placements, Whitney High School became one of the top schools in the nation, drawing new families to Cerritos in search of the very best education for their children.

"The Golden Triangle" Gleams

Through the '90s, the city also continued its quest for "the very best." Most visibly, construction crews hammered away on what city leaders hoped would be a profitable new shopping destination: the Cerritos Towne Center.

Vestar Development Company of Scottsdale, Arizona, had been chosen to develop the forty-one-acre parcel, with the original plan being to create an upscale mall on the order of Newport's Fashion Island. City leaders envisioned well-heeled shoppers driving from miles away to open their wallets at Neiman Marcus and Saks Fifth Avenue. However, studies revealed not only that the upscale market was in a slump, but also that another stylish mall might compete with the city's very own Los Cerritos Center. Success, leaders soon conceded, would be found instead in groceries and garden tools.

Taking a cue from the more moderately priced shops already thriving in Cerritos, including Fedco, Gemco (later Target), Best, Sportmart, and Home Depot, city leaders settled on plans for an "outdoor mall" anchored by an enormous full-service Smith's Food King and one of the first Wal-Marts in the Los Angeles area. With their angular lines and façades of granite, limestone, ceramic tile,

Community Partners: City of Cerritos and ABC Unified School District

Cerritos has enjoyed an enduring partnership between the City of Cerritos/Cerritos Redevelopment Agency and ABC Unified School District, which have worked together to provide stellar recreational facilities for the community.

The tradition began in 1979 when the City/Agency contributed $1.2 million for the construction of the stadium at Gahr High School, as well as another $1.2 million for the construction of a second gymnasium for the campus. In return, ABCUSD contributed ten acres of land where the City/Agency built the Cerritos Olympic Swim and Fitness Center.

Later, the City/Agency invested $2.5 million more for the construction of the Community Gymnasium at Cerritos High School in 1995 and another $2.4 million in 1997 for the construction of the Community Gymnasium at Whitney High School. Both facilities are used by students during school hours and by the community after hours and on weekends for drop-in play, sports programs, tournaments, and special events.

The City/Agency investments have continued, providing our schools with new bleachers, track resurfacing, gym flooring, lighting, traffic signals, parking lot paving, and many other enhancements that have benefited both students and the community.

The Community Gymnasium at Cerritos High School is busy daily, with local athletes enjoying two full-size basketball courts, two volleyball courts, and six badminton courts. The gym is used for both drop-in play and city classes. Copyright Marcus Tate.

With its towering spires, glass elevators, and striking ceramic tiles, the Cerritos Center for the Performing Arts is equally wondrous inside. Its one-of-a-kind six-thousand-square-foot auditorium features a moveable stage, floor, ceiling, and seats that can be resized and rearranged into six different configurations, tailored to each performance. Copyright Marcus Tate.

and pastel stucco, the Towne Center's stores quickly took shape. Colorful beds of flowers brightened the bases of more than eight hundred trees planted in the parking lot. Local shoppers rejoiced at a grand opening ceremony that included live entertainment and laser light shows.

Cerritos Center for the Performing Arts

But the laser shows were nothing compared to what was next door: a towering performing arts complex unlike anything American theatergoers had ever seen.

Visions for the Cerritos Towne Center had always included a community theater, and by 1986, city leaders were ready to draw up their plans in ink. The problem was, no one was quite sure who should hold the pen. For several weeks, the city council debated firmly but politely over plans for the 8.8-acre site. Some felt Cerritos was the perfect locale for a large venue that could compete with the likes of the Long Beach Terrace Theater, Orange County Performing Arts Center, and the Los Angeles Music Center. Others preferred a more modest recital hall that could host graduations, community groups, and local entertainers. Everyone dreaded the thought of anemic audiences twiddling their thumbs in an enormous and expensive white elephant.

In swept Theatre Projects Consultants of London to calm these fears and turn them into spectacular visions. The consultants, first hired in 1983, regaled Cerritos leaders with photos and details on the Derngate Theatre in Northampton, England, where blocks of seats on rollers could be rearranged or removed completely, tailored to each performance. Nothing like it existed anywhere in the United States.

Taken by the concept, the council hired Barton Myers Associates of Los Angeles to design a similar marvel for Cerritos. By 1987, plans included not only a theater with flexible seating for six distinct configurations, but also a fifty-one-hundred-square-foot conference center and a two-hundred-seat theater with its own sound and lighting systems. By now, excitement had taken hold.

Outside, construction crews molded the 154,000-square-foot building into what would become a striking city landmark of glass walls, pink limestone, colorful ceramic tiles, and angular points and projections. Tall glass elevator towers, topped by pyramids and thin spires where colorful pennants danced in the wind, flanked the entrance.

Right: *Theatergoers revel in the Cerritos Center for the Performing Arts' dramatic lobby on opening night. With its stylish fireplace, soaring ceiling, and eye-catching artwork, the lobby has become a favorite spot for weddings, with brides making a memorable entrance down the elegantly curved staircase. Copyright Marcus Tate.*

Below: *One of the technological marvels at the Cerritos Center for the Performing Arts is a set of three ceiling panels that can be deployed to create the perfect acoustics for any performance. This is done with help from a twenty-seven-thousand-pound panel called "the flipper" that adjusts to various positions. Copyright Marcus Tate.*

Above: *The Cerritos City Council uses a gleaming pair of golden scissors to debut the city's newest jewel, the Cerritos Center for the Performing Arts. Pictured from left to right are Mayor Pro Tem John F. Crawley, Councilmember Grace Hu, Mayor Sherman R. Kappe, and Councilmembers Ann Joynt and Paul W. Bowlen.*
Right: *Legendary crooner Frank Sinatra provided the inaugural performance on opening night at the Cerritos Center for the Performing Arts.*

The majestic new facility hosted a stream of celebrities, including a visit from HRH Charles, Prince of Wales, who attended a performance of Henry VI *by the Royal Shakespeare Company in November 1994.*

After much anticipation, on January 9, 1993, Mayor Sherman Kappe, Mayor Pro Tem John F. Crawley, Councilmember Paul W. Bowlen, Councilmember Grace Hu, and Councilmember Ann Joynt welcomed visitors to a ribbon-cutting and dedication ceremony, kicking off a two-day open house that featured guided tours of the wondrous new facility. An unending line of astounded visitors, four and six across, walked wide-eyed through the meeting rooms, the lobby, up the curving staircase, and through the theater. More than six thousand visitors attended the event to tour the fantastic new theater.

The building was truly stunning, and now it was up to the city to secure a stunning lineup. With a budget of $4 million to entice some of the top names in entertainment, the city truly landed a legend. When the lights dimmed on opening night, Ol' Blue Eyes himself—Frank Sinatra—stepped onto the stage to greet a packed house of adoring fans. With nary an empty seat in the place, Sinatra crooned his classics for the next three nights, confirming the Cerritos Center for the Performing Arts a place among the Southland's top venues.

Catch the COW

While architects devised grand plans for one of the nation's top theaters across the street, planners at City Hall used their creativity for more practical purposes. With hard-earned sales tax revenue and suggestions from constituents, city leaders had shifted into overdrive to provide the best possible services for residents, including a citywide shuttle system.

By 1992, city Dial-A-Ride vans were providing transportation for the disabled and elderly to clinics, hospitals, and appointments. Los Angeles and Orange County bus lines also crossed the city on their way to Los Cerritos Center. What was missing was an in-town system that could transport Cerritos residents quickly and easily to the city's parks, shopping centers, Cerritos College, the Civic Center, and high schools.

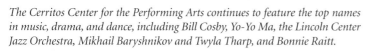

The Cerritos Center for the Performing Arts continues to feature the top names in music, drama, and dance, including Bill Cosby, Yo-Yo Ma, the Lincoln Center Jazz Orchestra, Mikhail Baryshnikov and Twyla Tharp, and Bonnie Raitt.

The Cerritos on Wheels (COW) buses were redesigned in 2005, with colored ribbons symbolizing movement and the "little hills" of the city's namesake. Routes were also redesigned to serve 110 stops throughout the city. The COW system now transports more than 160,000 passengers every year. Copyright Marcus Tate.

As planners mapped out routes and stops, City Hall launched a contest to name the new system. The winning moniker, devised by four separate winners, was clear: Cerritos on Wheels, or COW for short. The system took off running in August 1993, with rides priced at a quarter (now fifty cents), seven days a week, from 7:00 a.m. to 9:00 p.m.

A Center for Seniors

Soon there was a new stop on the COW route: the Cerritos Senior Center at Pat Nixon Park.

In neighborhoods across Cerritos, the mothers and fathers who had first brought their children to the city's new subdivisions were becoming grandparents. A good portion of the city's population was now over fifty, and yet, except for the city's Dial-A-Ride service, a food program at St. John's Lutheran Church, and the Gadabouts social club, not much was offered to this important group.

All that changed in 1994 with the opening of a $3.5 million, 22,500-square-foot clubhouse, built exclusively for the over-fifty set. First, the city settled on Pat Nixon Park as the site, for its central location. Next, Wolff, Lang, Christopher Architects Inc. was chosen to design a building very different from what had become the city's ultramodern style. Following the simple and homey Craftsman design, the Senior Center was constructed of wood framework and rustic river rock. Inside, the building offered two comfortable lounges, plus ample space for classes, arts and crafts, billiards, music listening, computers, and afternoon matinees. Its entrance featured an impressive tank swimming with exotic fish, while its World Hall offered space for special exhibits. A large multipurpose room provided a stage and catering kitchen, perfect for special celebrations. Outdoors, a park surrounded the building, with a patio and barbecue area, a Koi fishpond, and rolling lawns.

The center opened for business on January 29, 1994, offering a dizzying list of classes and activities, health screenings, a fitness center, tax and legal assistance, health and fitness workshops, excursions, and special events.

Rustic wood, vine-covered trellises, and river rock give the Cerritos Senior Center at Pat Nixon Park a comfortable, welcoming feel. A lush park, picnic grounds with a gazebo, and a patio with a colorful Koi pond surround the building. Copyright Marcus Tate.

The Cerritos Senior Center's five-thousand-square-foot Majestic Room and catering kitchen is frequently used for classes and special events, such as the center's annual Monte Carlo Night. Members of the community may also reserve the facility for adult-oriented events, such as weddings and anniversary celebrations. Copyright Marcus Tate.

Classes, activities, and trips are listed in the Cerritos Senior Center's bimonthly newsletter, "Senior Connection," which offers local seniors hundreds of activities to choose from. Here, a slithering yellow snake adds excitement to the center's annual Grandparents' Festival. Copyright Marcus Tate.

Cerritos Sheriff's Station/Community Safety Center

As local seniors finally had the facility they had long deserved, city leaders next turned their attention to securing Cerritos's position as one of the safest cities in the region.

Since its incorporation in 1956, Dairy Valley/Cerritos had worked closely with the Los Angeles County Sheriff's Department to ensure peace and safety for the city's residents and visitors. But, situated in the middle of one of the largest urban areas in the world, Cerritos was never immune to crime. City leaders hoped that a new station in the Civic Center would provide a stronger law enforcement presence plus convenience and more services for residents.

A site was selected sixty feet west of City Hall, and Pepper Construction of Irvine was chosen to build the $12.5 million facility. Graced by three fountains, the public entrance on the top floor would feature a spacious lobby capped by a skylight where residents would find assistance with everything from vacation security checks to overnight parking permits to children's fingerprinting and police reports. The top floor also housed a communications center, offices, and meeting rooms. The second floor became headquarters for nearly eighty

Graced by three bubbling fountains and decorative night lighting, the Cerritos Sheriff's Station/Community Safety Center stands as a symbol of safety and security for Cerritos residents and business owners. The facility opened in 1997, providing a full range of safety services twenty-four hours a day. Copyright Marcus Tate.

Thousands of residents enjoyed the grand opening of the Cerritos Sheriff's Station/Community Safety Center on March 8, 1997, an event that included tours, entertainment, refreshments, and special demonstrations and exhibits from the Los Angeles County Sheriff's Department. The ceremony was cablecast live on Cerritos TV3. Copyright Marcus Tate.

Cerritos sheriff's deputies stand at attention in front of the new Cerritos Sheriff's Station/Community Safety Center for a formal dress inspection by City and Sheriff's Department officials. The inspection was part of the facility's March 8, 1997, grand opening ceremony. Copyright Marcus Tate.

sheriff's deputies and support personnel, offering a training/briefing room, booking and custody areas, holding cells, lockers, and secured parking for sheriff's vehicles. As a later enhancement, the Cerritos Sheriff's Station/ Community Safety Center was upgraded to directly receive 911 emergency calls.

In addition to providing enhanced patrols and safety services to Cerritos twenty-four hours a day, seven days a week, the state-of-the-art facility offers a full range of services, including an active Volunteers on Patrol program, home and business security checks, a citywide Neighborhood Watch network, the Cerritos Crime Prevention Team, training programs, emergency preparedness workshops, and much more.

Affordable Housing for Seniors

While the Sheriff's Station was soon filled with deputies, volunteers, and the occasional arrestee, the city's newest project would be designed for residents of a very different sort: deserving seniors.

Left: Visitors at the community open house received a top-to-bottom tour of the new Cerritos Sheriff's Station/Community Safety Center. Here, residents check out the equipment in the building's dispatch center, which is charged with receiving 911 emergency calls and dispatching assistance. Copyright Marcus Tate.

Below: A new twelve-hundred-square-foot Cerritos Sheriff Community Safety Center is now open at Los Cerritos Center, serving as headquarters for mall deputies and providing crime prevention tips and children's fingerprinting for shoppers. Los Cerritos Center attracts up to fifty thousand daily visitors and seven million vehicles each year. Copyright Marcus Tate.

The first Cerritos affordable senior housing project opened in January 2000. Emerald Villas on Carmenita Road features a Mediterranean design with tile roofs, bubbling fountains, landscaped walking paths, and a clubhouse next to a spacious swimming pool and spa. Copyright Marcus Tate.

Compelled by state laws that required cities to invest a percentage of redevelopment revenue in affordable housing, Cerritos leaders devised a plan to subsidize the cost of top-quality condominiums, offering them for sale to some of the city's most venerable men and women. The units would be designated for longtime residents and their parents, ages sixty-two and older, with very low, low, and moderate incomes. The city acquired a six-acre plot on the west side of Carmenita Road, south of Coyote Creek, and, with help from The Lee Group, erected a 120-unit senior housing community named Emerald Villas. Well aware of the city's first-class style, more than twenty-four hundred potential buyers joined the waiting list, with the lucky few snapping up the one- and two-bedroom units ranging in price from $55,471 to $127,794. A second development, Pioneer Villas, was later dedicated in August 2001 on Pioneer Boulevard, one block north of Del Amo Boulevard, offering ninety-eight condominiums for sale to eligible seniors. Both communities offered a list of amenities and peaceful surroundings, with winding paths and plush landscaping.

But the high point of the city's senior housing program came in October 2002 with the opening of Avalon at Cerritos, a first-class congregate care facility built on Cerritos College land on the northeast corner of 166th Street and Studebaker Road. A unique partnership between the city, the college, and the developer, Vintage Senior Housing, LLC, the $14 million facility offers 147

Pioneer Villas, dedicated in August 2001 at Pioneer Boulevard and Eberle Street, was the second affordable senior housing complex to open, featuring ninety-eight condominiums for sale to eligible seniors ages sixty-two and older. The peaceful grounds are graced with palm trees, colorful flowerbeds, and a swimming pool and spa. Copyright Marcus Tate.

A dramatic fountain greets residents and visitors to Avalon at Cerritos. The City of Cerritos, Cerritos College, and Vintage Senior Housing, LLC, built the assisted living facility as a collaborative effort. Priority for residency goes to seniors who live in the Cerritos College District. Copyright Marcus Tate.

apartments plus daily meals, housekeeping, healthcare, and activities for very low, low, and moderate-income seniors (with some units available at market rates). The two-story Spanish Mediterranean–style facility also provides on-site multimedia and exercise rooms, a library, a hair salon, and a snack bistro. As part of this unique city-school partnership, the facility also serves as training grounds for Cerritos College students studying nursing, culinary arts, cosmetology, and horticulture.

A fourth affordable senior housing project is now in development, to be located on the southeast corner of 183rd Street and Carmenita Road. Following a Spanish-contemporary style of architecture, the eighteen-unit community will also feature a recreation building, extensive landscaping, decorative paving, and a major art piece.

Cerritos Library

While the city's senior housing projects were going up, another local landmark was coming down. With backhoes, jackhammers, and tractors, construction crews were demolishing the west half of the Cerritos Public Library by spring 2000 to make way for the project of the year: the new Cerritos Library.

By the turn of the twenty-first century, the library was one of the city's most popular attractions, drawing a throng of students, researchers, and readers seven days a week. Its books were in constant circulation, there were lines at the computer workstations, staff and volunteers scurried to restock shelves, and special programs were overwhelmingly well received.

At the same time, cities around the world were making plans for special events and projects to mark the new millennium. In Cerritos, the choice for a millennium project became clear, and as staffers quietly packed boxes and moved out of the library of the past, city leaders drew up plans for a towering library of the future.

Designed by Charles Walton Associates and built by C. W. Driver Contractors of Los Angeles, the $40 million Cerritos Library quickly took shape. The ambitious plans included space for three hundred thousand books, a plush conference center and warming kitchen, museum-quality displays, a High Tech Training Lab, and two hundred computer workstations. Pint-sized visitors would be amazed by a fifteen-thousand-gallon saltwater aquarium, a model

The towering Cerritos Library would become the first titanium-clad structure in the United States. Earth-friendly and maintenance-free, the titanium shell shows subtle color shifts as the angle of the sun and atmospheric conditions change throughout the day. Copyright Marcus Tate.

C. W. Driver Contractors demolished the west half of the Cerritos Public Library to make way for the three-story expansion. The crew drove 216 concrete piles fifty-four feet into the earth to anchor the building before pouring the building's foundation. Street sweepers and watering crews helped minimize dust for nearby residents. Copyright Marcus Tate.

The March 16, 2002, dedication of the expanded Cerritos Library included giveaways, refreshments, entertainment, a dinosaur "dig site," face painters, jugglers, and storytellers throughout the Civic Center. Revelers were issued wristbands to help organize tours of the building, which attracted more than nine thousand people. Copyright Marcus Tate.

"Main Street" inside Cerritos Library leads visitors to several destinations, including the Old World Reading Room stocked with rare first editions, and a "World Traditions" area featuring a large collection of print and multimedia resources in many languages. The library holds three hundred thousand books—more than five books per capita. Copyright Marcus Tate.

Immediately inside the Cerritos Library entrance, visitors are met with a fifteen-thousand-gallon saltwater aquarium that is stocked with colorful fish and sharks. An expert frequently conducts question-and-answer sessions from inside the aquarium, equipped with an underwater microphone. Copyright Marcus Tate.

of the space shuttle, a Tyrannosaurus Rex fossil replica, and a rainforest display. Adults could browse through a collection of more than 180,000 titles, plug their laptops into one of twelve hundred Internet ports, or relax by the fireplace with holographic flames in the Old World Reading Room.

Up a futuristic escalator, the library's second floor would offer computer stations, a Reference Desk, study rooms, and a "World Traditions" area with materials in dozens of languages and rotating exhibits spotlighting the city's cultural diversity. And at the top of a glass elevator, a third-floor conference center would provide one of the city's largest spaces for banquets, classes, teleconferences, and meetings. Throughout the library, Infostations would offer directions or quick assistance, while a high-tech radio frequency circulation system provided patrons with quick self-checkout.

On the day of its dedication, March 16, 2002, Mayor Paul W. Bowlen, Mayor Pro Tem Bruce Barrows, Councilmember John F. Crawley, Council-member Robert Hughlett, Ed.D., and Councilmember Gloria Kappe welcomed more than nine thousand eager patrons lined up for a first look, so many that color-coded wristbands were distributed to control the number of visitors admitted at one time. The festive celebration also included the release of white doves, refreshments, and children's activities.

"Stan," a full-sized replica of a Tyrannosaurus Rex fossil, is a popular character in the Children's Library, which also includes a model NASA space shuttle called "The Spirit of Cerritos," a lighthouse, a rainforest tree, an arts studio, and Little Theater. The ceiling is painted with a blue sky showing atmospheric changes. Copyright Marcus Tate.

Cerritos Library was named Best Public Library in 2004 by Reader's Digest, *which cited the library's titanium exterior, innovative customer service, and impressive children's area and computer stations. Forty million Americans read the magazine each month. Copyright Marcus Tate.*

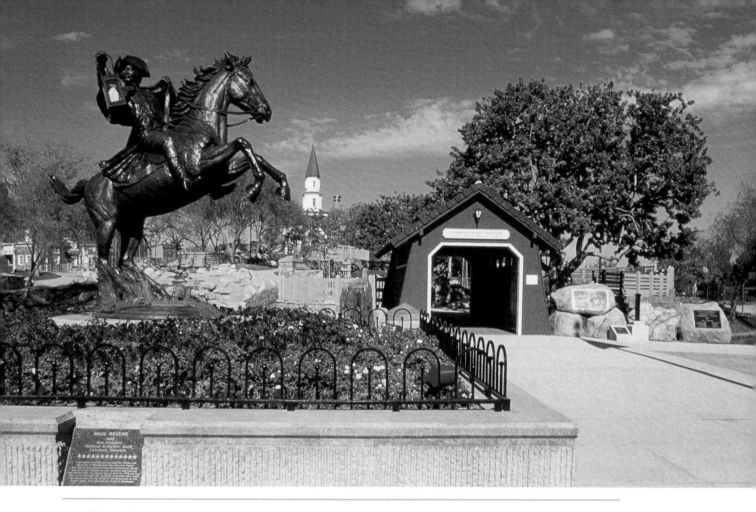

Part of the city's Art Work in Public Places program, the bronze sculpture of Paul Revere at Heritage Park was created by artist Dee Clements, a member of the National Sculptor's Guild. Installed in June 2002, the sculpture captures the bravery and patriotism of this famous Revolutionary War hero. Copyright Marcus Tate.

Hear Ye! Hear Ye! Heritage Park Reopens

As construction crews labored on the library of the future, another crew was perfecting visions from the past one block south on Bloomfield. Heritage Park Island, well loved by thousands of visitors over its twenty-five years, was receiving a well-deserved $5.3 million renovation with plans for a rebuilt eighteenth-century New England Village.

With help from David Volz Design and a committee of residents, the city's Parks and Recreation Commission had envisioned a unique play space, complete with a covered bridge, a sunken ship, cannons with buttons that made water geysers erupt in the lake, and a village with passageways, water features, slides, and cargo nets begging to be climbed. To the west, Boston Harbor beckoned with ships, a wharf, and colorful play equipment. Beyond a nine-foot-tall bronze statue of Paul Revere on horseback, young visitors could follow a series of signs around the island offering quotes from the Henry Wadsworth Longfellow poem "Paul Revere's Ride." To the south, visitors could

Toppled by a 1977 storm, this willow tree in Cerritos Civic Center is believed to be over one hundred years old, the last of a thicket described by writer Daniel Gridley in the 1880s. Now horizontal, the beloved tree survived the 2003 construction of Cerritos Library and an underground parking garage. Copyright Marcus Tate.

141

Unveiled in February 2005, the newly upgraded Liberty Park attracts more than three hundred thousand visitors every year. Copyright Marcus Tate.

enjoy a new "mini island" with a bandshell, designed for concerts, birthday parties, and special events.

Thousands of revelers enjoyed the grand opening on June 22, 2002, with guided tours, a Revolutionary War reenactment, educational exhibits, crafts, games, and entertainment.

Meanwhile, the city continued to add to its collection of parks every chance it got. In fall 2002, the city secured 5.25 acres of Southern California Edison property bordering the Coyote Creek Channel in eastern Cerritos and quickly laid out plans for a new neighborhood park. Less than four months later, residents celebrated the grand opening of El Rancho Verde Park, which featured meandering walkways, a botanical garden, a tot lot, exercise stations, and distance markers for power walkers.

Liberty Park Re-Dedication

With Heritage Park completed, city leaders soon set their sights across town on another popular park that was beginning to show its age. Since its opening in 1974, Liberty Park had attracted millions of visitors each year, with its amphitheater for summer concerts, track for runners and stroller-pushing parents, colorful playgrounds full of jubilant children, and picnic grounds busy with birthday parties and day camps—not to mention a bustling community center full of classes and activities. At thirty years old, it had been loved to death.

To restore Liberty Park to its original glory, the city hired KPRS Construction Services, Inc., to complete an $8 million north-to-south renovation. First on the priority list was a new, state-of-the-art eleven-thousand-square-foot community center, complete with a spacious multipurpose room, activity gallery, children's Discovery Depot, fitness center, lounge, and dance studio. Outside, visitors would find a new picnic shelter, a water play feature, a plaza area, sand volleyball courts, a rubberized 330-yard lighted track, and a renovated exercise cluster. Most impressive, the park would be home to new playgrounds, which would be completely accessible to children with disabilities. A life-size bronze sculpture of Abraham Lincoln was installed in front of the building, reminding visitors of the meaning behind the park's name.

Top: A partly submersed boat on the northwest tip of the Heritage Park Play Island is a popular spot for ducks and the children who like to feed them. The lake is also home to turtles and other wildlife. Copyright Marcus Tate.

Bottom: At just over five acres, the city's newest park, El Rancho Verde Park, offers picnic tables, a jogging and walking track, a botanical garden, par course stations, and colorful playground equipment. The neighborhood park is located at 7815 Denni Street. Copyright Marcus Tate.

Art Work in Public Places

When he was carefully installed in spring 2005, Honest Abe became the most recent addition to an impressive collection of paintings, sculptures, and sketches—strategically located to invite attention—which had come to brighten nearly every corner of Cerritos. Public artwork had become the finishing touch on this beautiful city.

The collection was first inspired in 1993 by the city's most triumphant masterpiece, the Cerritos Center for the Performing Arts, which had stirred a new appreciation for art and culture throughout the community. With its unique beauty, which *Performance Magazine* called "the most sophisticated project we've seen in terms of architecture, technology and urban design," the building also impressed visitors with its collection of distinctive artwork housed inside. An ethereal blue glass sculpture called *The Four Circles*, by Jamie Carpenter, floats within the lobby skylight, while an intriguing bronze piece called *Float Tower*, by artist Mark Lere, was installed on the building's third floor.

Just as these master works added interest to the theater building, city leaders quickly realized that artwork could enliven and add beauty to civic, retail, and office developments citywide. Following cities around the world, Cerritos formally established an Art Work in Public Places program, with the

At the age of thirty, Liberty Park underwent a major renovation in 2004. Here, construction crews work under the summer sun on what will become a modernized eleven-thousand-square-foot community center.

Three night-lighted sand volleyball courts at Liberty Park provide a fun place to challenge opponents and practice moves without a drive to the beach. Copyright Marcus Tate.

Liberty Park's 330-yard night-lighted track is popular among local runners and fitness walkers, many of whom meet up with friends after work for group exercise sessions. Copyright Marcus Tate.

One of the first installments in the city's Art Work in Public Places program, The Joy of Music *was unveiled on December 14, 1996, near the Cerritos Center for the Performing Arts. The bronze statue by Colorado artist George Lundeen depicts two singing children backed by three musicians. Copyright Marcus Tate.*

mission to create "a cultural legacy for future generations through the collection and exhibition of high-quality art pieces that reflect diverse styles, chronicling history through the collection of artifacts, documents and memorabilia that will acknowledge the past." A five-member Fine Arts and Historical Commission was formed to develop the program.

Today, with the cooperation of property owners and developers, the city's Art Work in Public Places program encompasses more than forty pieces, including sculptures, drawings, paintings, and water features with both abstract forms and realistic depictions of people and wildlife. The diverse collection contains works created with everything from fused and slumped glass, to cast bronze, watercolor and ink on rice paper, hand-carved ceramic tiles, blown glass and steel, and acrylic on canvas. Up to twenty more pieces will be added beginning in 2006 with the completion of a beautifully landscaped sculpture garden planned to grace the Cerritos Civic Center.

Opposite page: *Local developers have included public art pieces in their building designs. Luminaire, a bronze work by Colorado artist Denny Haskew, a member of the National Sculptor's Guild, was installed at the Transpacific Development Company office building at Cerritos Towne Center in August 2002. Similar contributions can be seen citywide. Copyright Marcus Tate.*

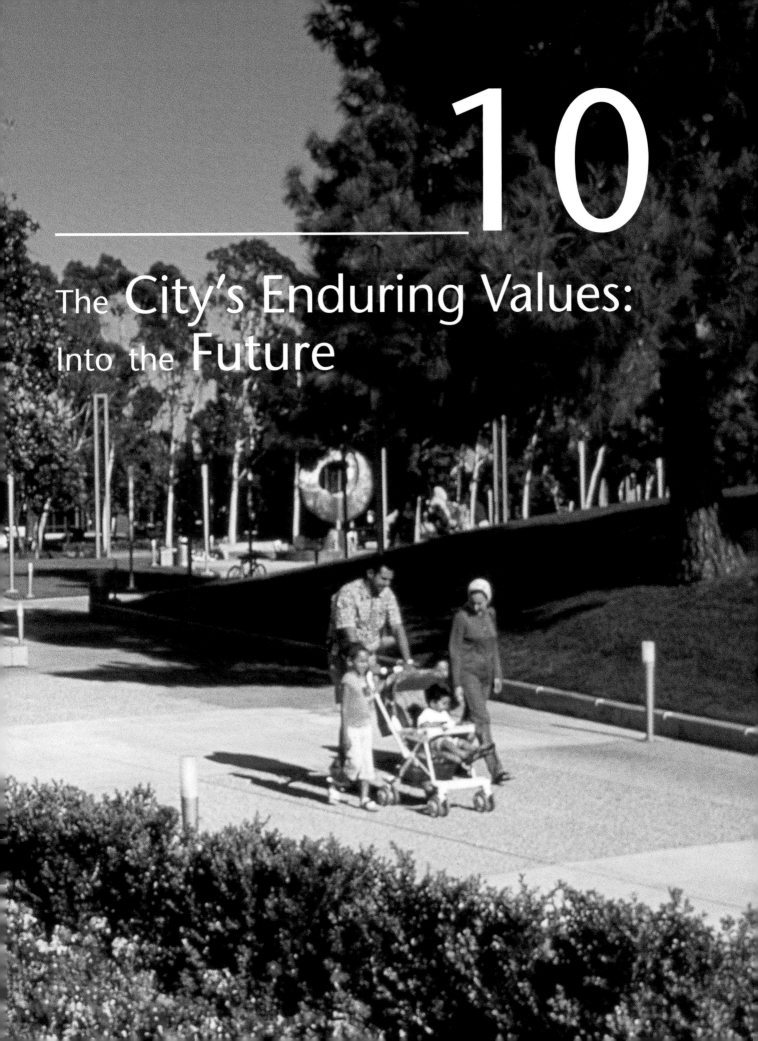

10

The **City's Enduring Values:**
Into the **Future**

*I*t's a typical sunny afternoon in Cerritos 2006. Two young mothers push strollers down a tree-lined street to their neighborhood park. Two Volunteers on Patrol cruise by, thankfully noting the peace and quiet. A few blocks east, a lively group of seniors greet each other with stories about their weekend exploits and then sit down for a workshop at the Cerritos Senior Center at Pat Nixon Park. The final bell rings at Cerritos High School, and a river of students flows north across 183rd Street for a homework session at Cerritos Library. A Cerritos on Wheels bus pulls up to the Civic Center, gathering passengers for an afternoon trip to the mall.

Along Studebaker Road, an excited college student pulls her parents through the dealerships at Cerritos Auto Square, kicking the tires of a car she hopes to call her own. At 5:00 p.m., the high rises at Cerritos Towne Center begin releasing their well-dressed occupants after a long day of work, many of whom head out to gatherings at nearby restaurants. A wife straightens her husband's collar and then flips through her wallet to make sure her tickets to the Cerritos Center for the Performing Arts are still there. In homes throughout the city, families are joining together once again, enjoying the end of another sunlit day.

The sights in Cerritos have certainly changed over the past five decades. The cows and sugar beets, drug stores, and dusty roads of Dairy Valley are gone. But as residents have come to understand, the qualities that define this beautiful city have endured. Since its incorporation in 1956, Cerritos has never strayed from the key values that continue to sustain and inspire our community.

Top: *Once the most diverse city of its size in the United States, Cerritos continues to be home to residents with a vibrant mix of backgrounds, ethnicities, and ages. Copyright Marcus Tate.*

Bottom: *Purple petunias are in bloom as a family takes a stroll through Cerritos Civic Center. The manicured grounds are home to Cerritos City Hall, Cerritos Library, the Cerritos Sheriff's Station/ Community Safety Center, and a new sculpture garden. Copyright Marcus Tate.*

Financial Security and Self-Reliance

While its ideal location has confirmed Cerritos as one of the Southland's top commercial centers, the city's position on the map isn't the only factor that led to its success. Experts will agree that, since their very first meetings, city leaders have been extraordinarily shrewd, carefully laying out a future of prosperity, security, and service that few other cities enjoy. From nine square miles of dusty cow pastures, city leaders artfully crafted a community that was able to sustain itself, with the largest auto mall in the world, a thriving light industrial center, and vibrant shopping centers injecting millions of dollars into the local economy.

While mom holds tight, little ones try their hand at feeding the ducks at Heritage Park. Picnic grounds, rolling lawns, colorful flowerbeds, and tranquil lakes can be found throughout the city, providing the perfect locales for relaxation.

Cheered on by his famly, a golfer takes aim on the Cerritos Iron-Wood Nine Golf Course. Copyright Marcus Tate.

Cerritos Towne Center has become one of Southern California's prime commercial, recreational, and business centers, with a roster of top tenants and retailers drawing millions of visitors each year. At the same time, the Cerritos Center for the Performing Arts continues to prove itself as one of the nation's top entertainment venues, offering 150 performances to delighted fans last year alone. All totaled, the bustling center is now producing annual retail sales in excess of $200 million. On the west side of town, Los Cerritos Center has earned its spot among Southern California's most outstanding upscale regional malls. Thanks to continuing rejuvenation and the ongoing addition of top-name boutiques by its ownership group, the Macerich Corporation, the Los Cerritos Center continues to boast annual sales of more than $350 million. And in 2005, the city's Cerritos Auto Square, a twenty-five-year-old institution, for the first time celebrated $1 billion in automotive sales, a testament to the center's unequaled location, reputation, and selection.

These strategic developments have proved invaluable to the community. They have provided thousands of jobs and millions of dollars in salaries for local families. They have helped buffer Cerritos from the ups and downs of the state and federal budgets and have provided protection from the financial woes other cities have endured. They have allowed the city to operate well in the black for five decades, asking very few fees or taxes of its residents. Most important, they have allowed Cerritos to provide a level of security, service, facilities, and programs for its residents that is unmatched.

An Appreciation for Business

Realizing that a strong economy is central to the city's success, Cerritos has devoted unwavering support to its business community. First and foremost, through its General Plan, the city has provided for a variety of modern office, retail, and light manufacturing facilities, tucked away from residential neighborhoods, that provide a perfect locale for nearly any enterprise. In addition to beautiful surroundings, well-kept streets, and a superior location, Cerritos provides personal attention to existing and potential business owners. A city ombudsman gives one-on-one support, helping entrepreneurs find suitable property, quickly secure permits, and open prosperous new facilities.

With its dramatic spray, the central fountain at Cerritos Towne Center has become a popular place to meet friends for an afternoon of shopping. Copyright Marcus Tate.

At Cerritos Auto Square, shoppers can view the products and talk with sales staff at their choice of twenty-one dealerships, all located within easy walking distance.

As of 2005, the Cerritos Auto Square employs nearly two thousand local residents and sells and leases more than sixty thousand vehicles each year, with sales topping $1 billion. A penny on every dollar spent on vehicle purchases is returned to the city as sales tax revenue, supporting parks, libraries, public safety, and other programs.

Cerritos city leaders lured popular purveyor Trader Joe's to the Cerritos Towne Center in the late 1990s. Now boasting two hundred stores, the chain offers more than two thousand grocery items, "all at honest everyday low prices." Copyright Marcus Tate.

Top: Opened on September 9, 1999, the seven-story AT&T Wireless Services headquarters at the Cerritos Towne Center became Southern California's first wireless office building. Advanced technology allows wireless phone, fax, and computer connectivity throughout the building, including in hallways and elevators. The company was later sold to Cingular. Copyright Marcus Tate.

Left: A full renovation of Los Cerritos Center in 1994 included new skylights, marble and stone walkways, new decorative benches, and interior landscaping. Mall shops were also organized into themed clusters called "The Garden," "The Grand Hall," and "The Avenue."

Newly opened at the corner of South Street and Gridley Road where a Fedco previously stood, South Street Cerritos is a lively shopping center with an Italian village theme. The center features numerous eateries, salons, clothing stores, and more. Adjacent is Target Greatland. Copyright Marcus Tate.

During an annual "Shop Cerritos" campaign, the City and Chamber of Commerce team up to promote the great fun, variety, and convenience of shopping within Cerritos city limits. Not only has the campaign succeeded in boosting sales tax revenue for city services, it has benefited retailers, both large and small, throughout the nine-square-mile city.

This unusual climate spurred *California Business Magazine* to name Cerritos one of the one hundred best places to do business in the state. And today, hundreds of companies who call Cerritos home, including United Parcel Service, Cingular Wireless, Delta Dental, Xerox Corporation, and ADP, would certainly agree.

Park-Like Surroundings

Drive from a neighboring town into Cerritos city limits and you'll immediately notice a change. Past the elegant monuments marking your entry into the City of Cerritos, you'll find smooth streets paved in rich black and not

a power line in sight to mar your view. Walls built to enclose the city's residential neighborhoods are now expanses of green, covered with carefully manicured creeping fig and Boston ivy. Sidewalks meander by beds of daylilies and agapanthus, next to upscale bus benches branded with the city logo. High schools are surrounded not by chain link, but by handsome wrought iron and feathery shrubs. More than thirty thousand city trees shade our streets and parks, with flowering plums releasing a snow of white petals each February and jacarandas jarring passersby with their neon purple blooms each spring. Near the city's major civic and retail centers, waterfalls cascade over rock formations into serene pools that regularly attract families of mallards. Streets are swept weekly, trees are trimmed by the calendar, and graffiti is scrubbed away overnight.

Cerritos undoubtedly has the "park-like look" early leaders had envisioned, and its beauty has become a significant source of community pride. While eyebrows have been raised through the years at the city's strict design guidelines and property maintenance codes, few would deny that these rules have served us well, attracting residents, businesses, and visitors alike. With a steady vision and outstanding support from property owners, at fifty, Cerritos is truly one of the best-looking cities in Southern California.

Top: *City crews maintain more than thirty thousand trees in city parks and along sidewalks and street medians, adding to the community's park-like appearance.*
Bottom: *City leaders instituted a "House of the Year" award in 2004 as part of the City Wide Pride program. Homeowners Michael and Diane Wheatley accepted the honor for their beautiful home on Chaparral Way. Copyright Marcus Tate.*

Education and the Arts

But, as everyone knows, looks aren't everything. Since the days when Dairy Valley's farm children filed down dusty dirt roads to Artesia Grammar School, the community has placed a premium on education and the arts. Today, ABC Unified School District is known statewide as a leader in educational planning and innovation, earning county, state, and national recognition for its outstanding programs. Cerritos College marked its fiftieth anniversary in 2005, offering degrees and certificates in eighty-seven disciplines, with more than twelve hundred students successfully completing their coursework each year.

The city's twenty-five-hundred-square-foot water-saving demonstration garden, located in the southeast section of Cerritos Park East, displays more than forty varieties of drought-tolerant trees, ground cover, and shrubs that thrive on very little water. Copyright Marcus Tate.

Cerritos Library is equipped with two hundred computer workstations and twelve hundred Internet ports. Patrons can search the on-line card catalog, explore the Internet, or research an infinite number of topics using the library's collection of on-line databases. Copyright Marcus Tate.

Part of the city's Art Work in Public Places program, Funny Papers *depicts a youngster relaxing with his favorite reading material. The bronze piece by Jane DeDecker, a member of the National Sculptor's Guild, was installed at the Centerstone housing tract in June 2001. Copyright Marcus Tate.*

Through the years, Cerritos city leaders have shown their dedication to schools through special programs, cultural activities, funding for recreational facilities, services and personnel from the Cerritos Sheriff's Station/ Community Safety Center, and much more. The Cerritos Library itself stands as a monument to lifelong learning, offering an unparalleled selection of books, periodicals, and electronic resources to students and researchers seven days a week, as well as a long list of educational programs and museum-quality exhibits for patrons of all ages. More than twenty-two hundred children join Cerritos Library's summer reading program each year, and more than twenty-six thousand patrons take part in programs ranging from children's story hours to hands-on computer training. All totaled, more than 1.2 million visitors are expected to walk through the library's towering doors this year alone, walking out with the gift of knowledge.

The Cerritos Center for the Performing Arts not only entertains but also brings a diverse world of drama, dance, and music to Cerritos audiences. Much effort goes into planning each season's lineup, with an emphasis on presenting performers and genres from around the globe. At the same time, the volunteer-driven Friends of Arts Education at the Cerritos Center for the Performing Arts touches children throughout the community with special school curricula and artists-in-the-classroom programs, dozens of free daytime performances, teacher workshops, and generous scholarships. The group now serves more than 120,000 students, teachers, and families each year from more than twenty-two Southern California school districts.

The lake at Cerritos Regional County Park is the site for the city's annual Kids' Fishing Derby, co-sponsored by the Cerritos Rod and Gun Club, which challenges local youngsters to catch "the big one."

Residents with disabilities and seniors can enjoy curb-to-curb transportation for just $1 a trip with Cerritos Dial-A-Ride. Reservations may be made twenty-four hours in advance by calling (866) 402-RIDE.

As this book goes to press, a five-thousand-square-foot expansion of the Cerritos Senior Center at Pat Nixon Park is underway. A new wellness/fitness center will help the city's active seniors stay healthy.

In addition, Cerritos's Art Work in Public Places program will be showcased at a new $1.8 million sculpture garden at the Cerritos Civic Center. The garden will incorporate lush landscaping, ample seating areas, abundant shade, and space for some twenty sculptures that will be added over time. The first two pieces to be installed will be a memorial to the victims of the 1986 Cerritos air disaster and the *Statue of Freedom*, a scaled reproduction of the sculpture that is displayed atop the United States Capitol building in Washington, D.C. The expansion of the Cerritos Senior Center and the new sculpture garden are gifts to the community in celebration of the city's fiftieth anniversary.

Safety and Service

Above and beyond its beautiful facilities, Cerritos continues to take pride in the exceptional level of service it offers. Once settled into the 90703 zip code,

160

Cerritos' streets are swept weekly to help keep neighborhoods tidy. Home maintenance guidelines and an active code enforcement program help keep Cerritos neighborhoods safe and attractive. Copyright Marcus Tate.

Cerritos residents and business owners are soon accustomed to quick responses, impeccably maintained streets, convenient transportation via Cerritos on Wheels, and many more advantages.

The city's Public Works Department is vigilant in maintaining the city's safety and appearance, taking responsibility for streets and lighting, tree care, traffic signals and signage, street sweeping, refuse collection and recycling, storm drains and sewers, water production and distribution, and the superior maintenance of all municipal facilities, fleet vehicles, medians, and parkways. At the same time, for the benefit of all residents and property owners, the city's Community Development Department keeps a firm grip on strategic planning and development, land use, and building and safety programs.

The city's Recreation Services Division offers an unending menu of classes, activities, and sports leagues for residents of all ages at twenty-one parks and facilities. Residents have their choice of three major community centers, a multiuse sports complex, a spacious executive golf course, two community gymnasiums, and an Olympic-quality swim center, not to mention quiet green parks within walking distance of nearly every home. More than a quarter of a million people, from tiny tots to seniors, take part each year in the city's sports, arts, crafts, dance, drama and special interest classes, clubs, adaptive programs, and excursions. The Cerritos Senior Center at Pat Nixon Park offers similar perks to residents ages fifty and up, hosting nearly fifty thousand special events and classes each year.

Top Left: *Two budding floral designers practice their skills at a city class. The city's Recreation Services Division offers thousands of fitness, dance, music, swimming, and special interest classes every year for residents of all ages. Copyright Marcus Tate.*

Top Right: *Located at the Cerritos Sports Complex, a ten-thousand-square-foot skate park was built for local skateboarders, featuring fun benches, ramps, rails, and curbs, plus pyramids, snake runs, hips, and bowls. A committee of Cerritos youths and adults helped design the park, which was built by Hondo Company, Inc. Copyright Marcus Tate.*

Left: *A stylish swinger takes a break from playing at Heritage Park. The play island's North Church steeple is shown in the background. Copyright Marcus Tate.*

Cerritos sheriff's deputies pride themselves on a community-based policing approach, with patrol deputies truly getting to know the residents and neighborhoods they serve. Active citizens help safeguard the city through Neighborhood Watch, Volunteers on Patrol, and Virtual Block Club programs. Copyright Marcus Tate.

In addition to providing quick response to emergency calls twenty-four hours a day, the Cerritos Sheriff's Station/Community Safety Center offers a multitude of services to residents on a walk-in basis, from children's fingerprinting and safety programs to parking permits, animal control services, and crossing guards. Thanks to ongoing communication with residents and business owners, a web site full of crime prevention information, one of the most advanced Virtual Block Club networks in the Southland, increased patrols at the city's major shopping centers, and active tracking and analysis of crime trends, the Cerritos Sheriff's Station has succeeded in suppressing crime and safeguarding the community's streets.

To make sure residents are fully aware of the services available to them, the city runs an active public information office that disseminates news through every avenue possible. The city's monthly newsletter, the *Cerritos News*, has become an institution, offering residents the latest news on city programs,

The City of Cerritos web site attracts as many as 37,482 visitors per month who view some 196,845 pages and log up to 225,677 hits.

Smiling children take a break from the summer heat in Cerritos Park East's popular spray pool. Copyright Marcus Tate.

Thousands of shoppers have come to frequent the Cerritos Certified Farmer's Market since its May 2001 opening at the Cerritos Towne Center. Set up on Park Plaza Drive, the market offers an amazing array of farm-fresh produce, eggs, seafood, bread, nuts, and flowers every Saturday from 8:00 a.m. to noon. Copyright Marcus Tate.

policies, and services. In addition, the city delivers a full-color calendar annually to each doorstep, maintains a comprehensive City Line telephone information service, and updates daily an award-winning city web site with information on nearly every facet of the community. Cerritos TV3, available via cable and on-line, provides citizens access to Cerritos City Council and commission meetings, as well as original programming and a community bulletin board.

People with Heart

But one quality surpasses all others. When Dairy Valley first incorporated, cows and chickens outnumbered people thirty-to-one. Today, that "human element" has taken hold, and its people have become the city's finest attribute. Over the past fifty years, Cerritos has not only grown as a city, it has evolved into a true community of proud, caring people dedicated to the good of their shared hometown.

During the city's farming days, crops weren't the only things to take root. Cerritos's diversity blossomed. People from all backgrounds—Portuguese and Dutch, Anglo, Mexican American, Asian American, African American, and many

164

One of the city's long-standing community groups, officially named in 1980, the Cerritos Gadabouts meet every week at the Cerritos Senior Center at Pat Nixon Park, planning trips, tours, luncheons, and special events for its senior members. Copyright Marcus Tate.

more—worked side-by-side, studied desk-by-desk, browsed down the same store aisles, reveled at the same celebrations, and became fast friends. By the late 1980s, a study by California State University, Northridge, confirmed Cerritos as the most ethnically diverse place in the United States, with more than eighty-four national and ethnic groups represented. Over time, this great diversity has grown even stronger. The 2000 U.S. Census reported that, of those who reported one race, 58.4 percent of Cerritos residents were of Asian descent (the largest groups being Chinese, Korean, Filipino, and Indian), 26.9 percent were Caucasian, 6.7 percent were black or African American, 0.3 percent were American Indian or Alaskan Natives, and 0.2 percent were Native Hawaiian or Pacific Islanders. Unlike other cities that are plagued by racial strife, Cerritos has become a striking example of camaraderie that is evidenced daily in every school and park, at every special event, at every shopping center—in every corner of the city.

Cerritos has also been blessed by its residents' deep involvement in the community. Not only is Cerritos fortunate to have an active and progressive city council, which gives voice to the city's diverse residents, citizens have the opportunity to serve on seven different advisory bodies. These consist of the Economic Development Commission, Fine Arts and Historical Commission,

The city's annual Summer Entertainment Showcase attracts thousands of patrons every year with a slate of after-dark movies, family shows, children's entertainers, concerts, and swim-in movies all summer long. Here, a pooch enjoys the best seat in the house at a Heritage Park concert. Copyright Marcus Tate.

165

Planned by the Let Freedom Ring Committee, the city's annual Independence Day celebration is fun for the entire family. Copyright Marcus Tate.

The Cerritos community is rich with dancing, singing, musical, and other performance groups show-casing cultures from around the world. Many are featured at the city's annual Festival of Friendship held each February at Los Cerritos Center. Copyright Marcus Tate.

the Parks and Recreation Commission, Planning Commission, and Property Preservation Commission, as well as the Community Safety Committee and Let Freedom Ring Committee. These important groups continue the city's early vision of "government by the people." In addition, Cerritos is now home to well over two hundred community groups, offering events, support, and camaraderie to thousands of residents of all ages. These diverse organizations include everything from Boy Scout and Girl Scout packs to cultural clubs, senior groups, professional and philanthropic associations, and sports leagues.

And just as Dairy Valley's farm families looked forward to Independence Day fireworks over the fields, Cerritos residents have shown their love for wholesome, community gatherings that bring families and neighbors together. Starting with the annual Festival of Friendship each February, featuring a 5K run, entertainment, and cultural displays at Los Cerritos Center, residents can count on at least one celebration each month, including grand openings and dedications, a Community Spring Festival, the annual Let

Fresh-faced singers entertain the crowd during the Let Freedom Ring Musical Production on Independence Day 2001 at Cerritos Park East. Copyright Marcus Tate.

Three young adventurers spend the afternoon hopping stones and relishing childhood at the Heritage Park play island.

The City of Cerritos began a new tradition this decade by participating in the annual Tournament of Roses Parade in Pasadena. Pictured is the city's 2004 entry, entitled "Rhapsody in Blue." The city's award-winning floats are decorated by hundreds of volunteers working several thousand hours to perfect each creation. Copyright Marcus Tate.

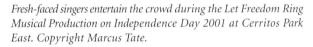

167

Freedom Ring Festival at Cerritos Park East, concerts and
children's shows throughout the summer, Halloween
festivals and pumpkin contests, a Veterans Day ceremony,
a holiday boutique, a tree-lighting ceremony, and more.
Regularly attracting tens of thousands of revelers, these
events have become a beloved tradition for Cerritos
families, passing the spirit of community and the joy
of simple pleasures on to new generations.

Fifty and Beyond

So it is no surprise that as the City of Cerritos
approaches its fiftieth birthday, the community is in for a
celebration like no other. The fledgling City of Dairy Valley
has successfully made its way to adulthood, with a distinct
personality, unwavering strengths, and an astounding list
of accomplishments none of its forefathers could have ever
imagined. At fifty, Cerritos is a remarkable community
of financial stability, caring residents, gracious homes,
world-class facilities, unparalleled service, and stunning
streetscapes—truly a city to celebrate. As we rejoice with
parades and festivals, souvenirs, and merriment, let us also
honor our past and recognize the fundamental qualities that
have brought us to 2006: hard work, vision, cooperation,
pride, and optimism.

It is to these strengths we owe our city's glorious future.
Happy birthday, Cerritos!

An aerial shot looking north past Cerritos Towne Center toward the San Gabriel Mountains shows the City of Cerritos' development. Copyright Marcus Tate.

Appendix 1

Dairy Valley/Cerritos City Council Members
1956 to present (in order of beginning service year)

Jacob N. Albers
1956–70 (Mayor
1959–60, 1965–66,
1970)

Jack R. Bettencourt
1956–59 (Mayor
1956–59)

Hal Rees
1956–60

Louis Struikman
1956–58, 1960–68
(Mayor 1962–63,
1967–68)

Albert Veldhuizen
1956–58

Alex Moore
1958–66 (Mayor
1960–61, 1964–65)

Joe A. Gonsalves
1958–62 (Mayor
1961–62)

Frank C. Leal
1960–71 (Mayor 1963–
64, 1968–69, 1971)

Frank Pinheiro
1963–64

Fred Troost
1964–70 (Mayor
1966–67)

Tony Cordeiro
1966–70 (Mayor
1969–70)

Patton D. Winslow
1968–70

Frank D. Lee
1970–78 (Mayor
1973–74)

Barry A. Rabbitt
1970–90 (Mayor
1972–73, 1975–76,
1979–80, 1984–85,
1988–89)

James S. Reddick
1970–78 (Mayor
1971–72, 1976–77)

Robert J. Witt
1970–71, 1972–78
(Mayor 1970–71,
1977–78)

James Pearce
1971–72

Dennis Bradshaw
1972–80 (Mayor
1974–75, 1978–79)

Alex H. Beanum
1978–86 (Mayor
1981–82)

Diana S. Needham
1978–90 (Mayor
1980–81, 1985–86,
1989–90)

Daniel K. Wong
1978–92 (Mayor
1983–84, 1987–88)

Don Knabe
1980–88 (Mayor
1982–83, 1986–87)

Ann B. Joynt
1986–94 (Mayor
1990–91)

Paul W. Bowlen
1988–97, 1999–
present (Mayor
1991–92, 1994–95,
2001–02)

John F. Crawley
1990–99, 2001–
present (Mayor
1993–94, 1998–99,
2005–present)

Sherman R. Kappe
1990–99 (Mayor 1992–
93, 1996–97)

Grace Hu
1992–2001 (Mayor
1995–96, 1999–2000)

Bruce W. Barrows
1994–2003 (Mayor
1997–98, 2002–03)

Robert Hughlett, Ed.D.
1997–2005 (Mayor
2000–01, 2004–05)

Gloria A. Kappe
1999–present (Mayor
2003–04)

Laura Lee
2003–present

李欒復青

Jim Edwards
2005–present

Appendix 2

Dairy Valley/Cerritos City Managers

William Cecil	April 1956 to September 1956
Mayrant D. McKeown	September 1956 to March 1961
Bill Stark	April 1961 to June 1970
John DeWeerd	June 1970 to June 1973
Gaylord Knapp	June 1973 to April 1991
Art Gallucci	April 1991 to the present

Appendix 3

City of Cerritos Awards and Honors

Environmental Planning Award, Bettencourt Park

Award for Comprehensive Planning, Financial and Management Program from the University of Southern California (USC)—1973

Best Community Park in the State, Liberty Park   1975

Award of Merit for Excellence in Park and Recreation Management from the National Sports Foundation—1975

Energy Conservation Award, Planning Division—1975

Program Excellence Award for the Leisure Fair from the California Parks and Recreation Society—1982

Certificate of Achievement in Financial Reporting from the Government Finance Officers Association of the United States and Canada—1986–2004

Certificate of Award for Outstanding Financial Reporting from the California Society of Municipal Finance Officers—1986–2003

National Award of Excellence American Institute of Architects (AIA) and American Library Association (ALA) for Cerritos Public Library—1988

Award of Honor Southern California Institute of Architecture for Cerritos Public Library—1988

Merit Award for Excellence in Handicap Accessibility for Rosewood Park from the California Department of Rehabilitation—1988

Golden Shield Award for Outstanding Contribution to the Federation from the Southern California Municipal Athletic Federation—1988, 1993, 1998, 2003

Environmental Planning Award for Liberty Park from the California Parks and Recreation Society—1989

Special Award of Excellence—Best Community Park in the State for Liberty Park from the California Parks and Recreation Society and ARCO—1989

Cabrillo Chapter of American Institute of Architects Design Award for the Cerritos Center for the Performing Arts—1993

Concrete Industry Paving Award for the Cerritos Center for the Performing Arts—1993

Amusement Business magazine Top 10 Venues in the United States with 5,000 seats or less for the Cerritos Center for the Performing Arts—1993–2001

Los Angeles Business Council Kaufman and Broad Award for the Cerritos Center for the Performing Arts—1994

United States Institute of Theater Technology Honor Award for the Cerritos Center for the Performing Arts—1994

Performance Magazine "Theater of the Year" for the Cerritos Center for the Performing Arts—1995

City Hall Public Information Awards Competition Grand Award for Outstanding Video Production Achievement "Cerritos: The Place To Be"—1996

Helen Putnam Award from the League of California Cities for IMPACT (Intercepting Minors with Positive Attention, Care & Training), Public Safety, Award for Excellence—1997

Innovative Sports Program Award for the Cerritos Mayor's Cup from the Southern California Municipal Athletic Federation—1998

Outstanding Sports Facility Award for the Whitney High School Community Gymnasium from the Southern California Municipal Athletic Federation—1998

City-County Communications and Marketing Association Savvy Award for Best Video "Every 15 Minutes"—1999

City-County Communications and Marketing Association Savvy Award for Best Technology Services World Wide Web—1999

Merit Award for Facility Design of the Cerritos Skate Park from the California Parks and Recreation Society—2000

Recognition from the California State Assembly for the Cerritos Saturday Marketplace—2001

Helen Putnam Award for Excellence from the League of California Cities for Senior Housing (covering all senior housing projects and programs)—2001

Outstanding New Sports Facility Award for the Cerritos Skate Park from the Southern California Municipal Athletic Federation—2001

Innovative Sports Program Award for the Cerritos Skatefest Series from the Southern California Municipal Athletic Federation—2001

Achievement Award for the Family Entertainment Showcase from the California Parks and Recreation Society—2002

Senior Achievement and General Excellence (SAGE) Award from the Seniors Housing Council of the Building Industry Association of Southern California for Avalon at Cerritos—2002

California Association of Park and Recreation Commissioners and Board Members Special Award—2002

California State Assembly Recognition for the Festival of Friendship—2003

Outstanding New Sports Facility Award for the Cerritos Sports Complex from the Southern California Municipal Athletic Federation—2003

Outstanding New Sports Program Award for the Cerritos Sports Extravaganza from the Southern California Municipal Athletic Federation—2003

Special Congressional Recognition for Service to the Community by the Let Freedom Ring Committee—2003

Tournament of Roses Parade Judges' Special Trophy for "Reading Can Be Magical" float—2003

Themed Entertainment Association Thea Award for Cerritos Library—2003

Cerritos Library designated Best Public Library by *Los Angeles Magazine*—2003

EXPY Award (Experience Stager of the Year) for Cerritos Library—2003

Tournament of Roses Parade Craftsman Trophy for "Rhapsody in Blue" float—2004

Cerritos Library denoted Best Public Library by *Reader's Digest* Best of America issue—2004

Tournament of Roses Parade Tournament Special Trophy for "Families Make A Community" float—2005

Helen Putnam Award from the League of California Cities for Public Works, Infrastructure, and Transportation—Honorable Mention (awarded by the League of California Cities) for Cerritos Transit Services (COW and Dial-A-Ride)—2005

Telly Award Finalist for Video Production "The Art of the Cerritos Library"—2005

California State Assembly Recognition for the Re-dedication of Liberty Park—2005

Community Problem Solving/Team Building Award to the Parks and Recreation Commission for Adaptive Programs from the National Recreation and Parks Association—2005

Bibliography

ABC Unified School District Archives, Cerritos Public Library History Collection.

An Illustrated History of Los Angeles County California. Chicago: Lewis Co., 1885.

Bancroft, Hubert H. *History of California Vol. 2—California Pastoral.* Santa Barbara, CA: Wallace Hebberd, 1966 ed.

Bauer, Helen. *California Indian Days.* Garden City, NY: Doubleday and Co., 1968.

Bauer, Helen. *California Rancho Days.* Garden City, NY: Doubleday and Co., 1968.

Berner, Loretta. *Rancho Los Cerritos.* Ramona, CA: Acoma Books, 1975.

California Atlas. Culver City, CA: Pacific Book Center, 1979.

Caughey, John W. and Norris Hundley. *California—History of a Remarkable State.* Englewood Cliffs, NJ: Prentice Hall, 1982.

Cerritos Auto Square web site. http://www.cerritosautosquare.com, 2005.

Chartkoff, Joseph and Kerry K. Chartkoff. *Archeology of California.* Stanford, CA: Stanford University Press, 1984.

City of Artesia. "Artesia's History." City of Artesia web site. http://www.cityofartesia.us/history.html.

City of Cerritos. City of Cerritos web site. http://www.ci.cerritos.ca.us.

"The City of Cerritos." *South Coast Business*, 1986. CPL Local History Collection.

City of Cerritos Combined Financial Program: 2004–2005. City of Cerritos, 2004.

Cleland, Robert Glass. *Cattle on a Thousand Hills.* San Marino, CA: Huntington Library, 1941.

Crouch, Winston W. and Robert N. Giordono. "The Example of Dairy Valley." *A Place to Live—The Yearbook of Agriculture.* U.S. Department of Agriculture, 1963.

Crump, Spencer. *Henry Huntington and the Pacific Electric.* Corona del Mar, CA: Trans-Anglo Books, 1978.

Dana, Richard Henry, Jr. *Two Years Before the Mast.* New York: Harper Row, 1958.

Dary, David. *Cowboy Culture: A Saga of Five Centuries.* New York: Albert A. Knopf, 1981.

Dumke, Glenn S. *The Boom of the Eighties in Southern California.* San Marino, CA: Huntington Library, 1944.

Durrenberger, Robert W. *Patterns on the Land.* Palo Alto, CA: National Press Books, 1974.

Eisenhower, Julie Nixon. *Pat Nixon, the Untold Story.* New York: Simon and Schuster, 1986.

Electric Railway Historical Association of Southern California web site. http://www.erha.org.

Gahr High School History Honors Class, Carl Rogers, Advisor. "Cerritos, a Short History." Class project, 1978.

Groeling, John Carman. "A Historical Study of the Early Development of Bellflower, California." Master's thesis, Whittier College, 1954.

Guinn, J. M. *A History of California and an Extended History of Los Angeles and Environs, Vol. I.* Los Angeles: Historic Record Co., 1915.

Hansen, Harry, ed. *California, a Guide to the Golden State.* New York: Hastings House, 1967.

Johnson, Paul C., ed. *The California Missions.* Menlo Park: Lane Book Co., 1964.

Kahanek, Richard L. *A History of Norwalk.* City of Norwalk, 1968.

Kroeber, A. L. *Handbook of the Indians of California.* New York: Dover Publications, 1976.

Lavender, David. *California—Land of New Beginnings.* New York: Harper & Row, 1972.

Little, Al. *The Artesians—How it Began 100 Years Ago.* Lakewood, CA: Advocate, 1975.

Little, Albert O., comp. *Images of America: Artesia 1875–1975.* Edited by Veronica L. Bloomfield and Veronica E. Bloomfield. Charleston, SC: Arcadia Publishing, 2000.

Los Angeles County, Economic Resource Profile. New York: Impressions, Inc., 1988.

Los Cerritos Center web site. http://www.shoploscerritos.com.

McWilliams, Carey. *California—The Great Exception.* New York: A. A. Wyn, 1949.

McWilliams, Carey. *Southern California, an Island on the Land.* Santa Barbara, CA: Peregrine Smith, 1973.

Miller, Crane S., and Richard S. Hyslop. *California—The Geography of Diversity.* Palo Alto, CA: Mayfield Publishing Co., 1983.

Nava, Julian and Bob Barger. *California—Five Centuries of Cultural Contrasts.* Beverly Hills, CA: Glencoe Press, 1976.

Nelson, Howard J. *Los Angeles Metropolis.* Dubuque, IA: Kendall/Hunt Pub. Co., 1983.

Ornduff, Robert. *Introduction to California Plant Life.* Berkeley, CA: University of California Press, 1974.

Quinn, Charles Russell. *History of Downey.* Downey, CA: Elena Quinn, 1973.

Reisenberg, Felix, Jr. *The Golden Road.* New York: McGraw-Hill, 1962.

Robinson, W. W. *Ranchos Become Cities.* Pasadena, CA: San Pasqual Press, 1939.

Rojas, Arnold R. *The Vaquero.* Santa Barbara, CA: McNally and Loftin, 1964.

Rolle, Andrew F. *California.* Arlington Heights, IL: Harley Davidson, Inc., 1978.

Schurz, William Lytle. *The Manila Galleon.* New York: E. P. Dutton, 1939.

Stamps, James L. and Mamie R. Kryth. *Historical Volume and Reference Works.* Arlington, CA: Historical Publishers, 1965.

U.S. Department of Commerce, Bureau of the Census. *County and City Data Book, 1983.*

Warren, John Quincy Adams. *California Ranchos and Farms.* Edited by Paul W. Gates. Madison, WI: State Historical Society of Wisconsin, 1967.

Wilson, John Albert. *Reproduction of Thompson and West's History of Los Angeles County, California.* Berkeley, CA: Howell-North, 1959.

Yonay, Ehud. "Where Have All the Cows Gone?" *Westways,* March 1971.

Newspapers:

Bellflower (CA) Herald American

Cerritos News (city newsletter)

Cerritos Sun

Community Advocate

Los Angeles Times

News Tribune

Long Beach Press-Telegram

(Clippings from the above publications are available in the Cerritos Library Local History Collection)

-A-

ABC Adult School, 90

ABC Unified School District, 72, 88, 100, 121, 157

Air disaster, 73, 108–109, 160

Aircraft industry, 40, 41

Albers, Jacob "Jim", 43, 46, 50, 54, 57, 62, 68, 69, 74

Alpha Beta grocery store, 67, 68

Art Work in Public Places, 141, 144, 146, 159, 160

Artesia, 26, 27, 28, 30, 31, 33, 34, 35, 36, 37, 40, 42, 43, 44, 49, 56, 58, 67, 81, 84

Artesia Crest homes, 49, 56

Artesia, downtown, 29, 30, 31, 32, 44, 51, 56

Artesia Grammar School, 26, 31, 32, 34, 43, 44, 157

Artesia Zoned District, 42, 43, 46

Artesian wells, 26

AT&T Wireless Services building, 155

Automatic Data Processing (ADP), 109

Avalon at Cerritos, 134, 135

-B-

Banchaio, Taiwan, 73

Bandini, Arcadia, 23

Barbaria family, 60

Barton Myers Associates, 123

Beautification, 98, 118

Bengel, Margaret, 55

Best Plaza, 105

Bettencourt, Jack R., 46, 54

Bettencourt Park, 82

Bicentennial, 85

Bonelli, Frank, 57, 61, 62, 71

Broadway, 79

Brookhaven Park, 82

Brown, Jerry, 92

Business climate, 80, 106

-C-

Cable service, 110

Carmenita Junior High School, 88

Cattle ranching, 21

Cecil, William "Bill", 54, 55

Central Milk Producers Association, 46

Central Milk Sales, 54, 55

Cerritos, city name change, 73–74

Cerritos Auto Square, 49, 82, 93–95, 110, 113, 150, 152, 154

Cerritos Center for the Performing Arts, 109, 122, 123–126, 127, 144, 146, 150, 152, 159

Cerritos College, 57, 58, 90, 102, 105, 109, 126, 134, 135, 136, 157

Cerritos Corporate Tower, 105

Cerritos High School, 90, 121, 150

Cerritos Industrial Park, 90–91, 112

Cerritos Library, 72, 73, 82, 136–140, 141, 150, 158, 159

Cerritos Olympic Swim and Fitness Center, 102, 103, 121

Cerritos on Wheels (COW), 126, 128, 150, 161

Cerritos Park East, 82, 84, 85, 100, 102, 158, 167, 168

Cerritos Regional County Park, 84, 87, 105, 114, 160

Cerritos Senior Center at Pat Nixon Park, 51, 128–129, 150, 160, 161, 165

Cerritos Sheriff's Station/ Community Safety Center, 131–132, 150

Cerritos Sports Complex, 114, 115, 162

Cerritos Towne Center, 36, 104, 109, 111, 112, 119, 120, 121, 123, 146, 150, 152, 153, 154, 155, 164, 169

Chamber of Commerce, Cerritos, 75, 80, 105, 118, 156

Chamber of Commerce, Dairy Valley, 67, 73, 80

Chenevert, Mr. and Mrs. Marvin, 69, 70

City Hall, 58, 61, 69, 72, 91–92, 93, 98, 109, 119, 126, 128, 131, 150

City Wide Pride, 51, 118–119, 157

Commissions and Committees, 165–166

Community groups, 123, 165, 166

Community gymnasiums, 121, 161

Cordeiro, Tony, 57, 74

Corporate Yard, 93

Coyote Creek, 20, 33, 42, 46, 56, 82, 134, 143

Crops, 16, 18, 27, 30, 32, 33, 40, 44, 49, 164

-D-

Dairy industry, 27, 35–36, 43, 44, 46, 56, 58, 60, 66, 67

Dairy Valley City Council, 57, 62

Dairy Valley, boundaries, 46, 49

Dairy Valley, incorporation, 43, 46, 49

Dairy Valley, library, 60

Dairy, demolition, 110

De Campo, Francisco, 21

De Mello, Francisco, 46

De Voss Dairy, 85, 88

Deukmejian, George, 71, 74, 82

Dial-A-Ride, 126, 128, 160

Diversity, 98, 100, 101, 139, 164, 165

Dodgers, Los Angeles, 60

Douglas Aircraft Company, 40, 41

Dutch community, 36

-E-

Early explorers, 16

Earthquake, 1933 Long Beach, 32, 34, 35, 45

Ecology Park, 82

Edwards Stadium 10 Cinemas, 119

Elections, 49, 54, 55, 66, 74, 100

Emerald Villas, 134

Excelsior High School, 31, 34, 35, 44, 45, 83

-F-

Festival of Friendship, 166

Finances, 56, 120–121

Fire Station #30, 98, 99

"Fix Up, Clean Up" campaign, 55, 118

Fleishman, Maurice H., 81, 91

Flood control, 34, 72

Flooding, 33, 55, 56

Frampton, George, 27, 33

Franz, Myrtle, 51

Freeway buffer walls, 78

"Freeway City", 73

Freeway, Interstate 605, 45, 66, 74, 75, 85, 94, 95

Freeway, Santa Ana (Interstate 5), 30, 60

Freeway, State Route 91, 45, 63, 66, 70, 74, 102, 104, 105

Friends of the Library, 82

Friendship Park, 82

Funny Papers, 159

-G-

Gabrieleno Indians, 11–12, 13, 16

Gadabouts, 128, 165

Gahr High School, 71, 72, 88, 90, 121

Garnett, William A., 42

General Plan, 72–73, 93, 152

Golf Course, Iron-Wood Nine, 85, 89, 105, 151

Gonsalves, Joe A., 62, 72, 74, 75, 82

Gorinis family farm, 27

Government, form of, 42, 49, 55, 166

Gridley Park, 82

-H-

Hahn, Inc., Ernest W., 79

Hanford Rants Stadium, 88, 90

Hayes, James, 87

Heritage Park, 85, 88, 89, 141, 143, 144, 151, 162, 165, 167

Hickey, Agnes, 55

Horn, Joy D., 54

Housing boom, 40, 42

Huntington, Henry, 26, 27

-I-

Iacoboni, Angelo, 43

Itapetinga, Brazil, 73

-J-
Jacob Park, 82, 86
Jersey Gold Dairy, 67
Joy of Music, The, 146

-K-
Kids' Fishing Derby, 160
Knevelbaard Dairy, 94
Koopman Gas Station, 36

-L-
Lakewood, 19, 40, 42, 49, 56, 58, 74, 84
"Lakewood Plan", 42, 71
Lazy L Ranch, 63
Leal, Frank, 43, 57, 62, 68, 73, 74
Leandry, Francesca Uribe, 20–21
Leandry, Juan Bautiste, 20
Let Freedom Ring Celebration, 82, 166, 167
Liberty Park, 84, 85, 113–114, 115, 142, 143, 145
Lincoln Station, 110, 113
List, John, 55
Loma Park, 82
Long Beach, 12, 19, 20, 26, 27, 34, 40, 41, 42, 45, 51, 90
Long family, 63
Loreto, Mexico, 73
Los Angeles, 11, 21, 22, 23, 26, 27, 30, 35, 45, 51, 60, 90, 100
Los Cerritos Center, 79, 95, 98, 104, 121, 126, 133, 152, 155, 166
Los Cerritos Center, Community Safety Center at, 133
Luminaire, 146

-M-
McKeown, Mayrant "Mac", 55, 56, 58, 60
Miss Cerritos, 75, 79
Mission San Gabriel, 11, 17, 18
Monterey Acres, 49
Morgan, Stanley, 72
Motorcycle Park, 84, 87
Muñoz, Manuel, 112

-N-
Native Americans, 11, 12, 16, 18, 21
Neighborhood Watch, 51, 98, 132, 163

Nieto, José Manuel Pèrez, 19
Nixon Home and Museum, 85
Nixon, Pat, 31, 74, 82, 83
Nordstrom, 79, 98

-O-
Ohrbach's, 79
Olympic Games, 1984 Los Angeles, 100

-P-
Pacific Electric Railway, 26, 27, 30, 33, 45
Padelford, A. J., 81, 82
Palacio, El, 23
Park, planning, 82
Pat Nixon Park, 85, 128, 129, 150, 160, 161, 165
Pico, Andres, 22
Pinheiro, A. C., 46, 50, 54
Pioneer Villas, 134, 135
Portuguese community, 36, 37
Portuguese Hall, 37
Post office, 28, 42, 105, 106
Prince Charles, 126
Producers Livestock Marketing Association, 60
Public Works, 161

-Q-
Queen Juliana and Prince Bernhard, Netherlands, 36, 37

-R-
Ranchos, Life on the, 19
Ranchos, ownership, 20–23
Rancho La Buena Esperanza, 20
Rancho Los Cerritos, 19, 73
Rancho Los Coyotes, 20, 22
Rancho Los Nietos, 19
Rancho San Pedro, 19
Rancho San Rafael, 19
Reagan, Ronald, 74
Recreation classes, 161, 162
Red Cars, 26, 27, 30, 33
Redevelopment, 78, 79, 80, 85, 88, 90, 93, 94, 104, 105, 109, 110, 120, 121, 134
Rees, Hal, 46, 54
Reservoir Hill Park, 82, 86
Restaurant Row, 45, 98, 105
Rivers, 23, 33, 34
Road paving, 40, 55

Robinson Trust, 23
Robinsons, 79
Rose Parade floats, 167

-S-
Saddleback Park, 82
Schoneveld, John, 46
Schools, 34, 46, 49, 60, 70, 72, 83, 88, 90, 101, 105, 121, 126, 157, 159
Sculpture garden, 146, 150, 160
Sheriff, Los Angeles County, 72, 99, 131, 132
Senior housing, 132, 134–136
Sinatra, Frank, 125, 126
Sister Cities, 73
Solar power, 92, 93
Sears, 79
Serra, Father Junípero, 16, 17
Sewer project, 74
Sheraton Cerritos Hotel, 109, 110, 111, 119
"Shop Cerritos" campaign, 156
Sign ordinance, 80, 81
Special events, 85, 103, 114, 121, 129, 130, 136, 143, 161, 165
Sperou, George, 46
"Stan" the Tyrannosaurus Rex, 140
Stearns, Abel, 22, 23, 73
Summer Entertainment Showcase, 165
Sunshine Park, 82
Struikman, Louis, 46, 54, 62, 68, 70, 74

-T-
Thompson, O. J., 27, 33
Tongva Indians, 11, 13
Tracy High School, 90
Trader Joe's, 120, 154
Transpacific Development Company, 105, 110, 146
Treaty of Guadalupe Hidalgo, 22
Troost, Annie, 44–45
Troost, Fred, 45, 50, 57, 67, 68, 69, 70, 74

-U-
United Parcel Service (UPS), 91, 156

-V-
Veldhuizen, Albert, 43, 46, 54

Vineyards, 18, 19, 27
Volunteers on Patrol, 132, 150, 163

-W-
Walton Associates, Charles, 136
Water, infrastructure, 57
Water, waterfalls, 95, 104, 105, 113, 157
Water, recycled, 88, 98, 105
Water, reservoir, 31, 34, 69, 84, 86
Weather, 10, 33
Westgate Park, 82
Whitney Education Center, 90

-X-
Xerox, 90, 156

-Z-
Zoning, 58, 61, 66, 69, 80, 81

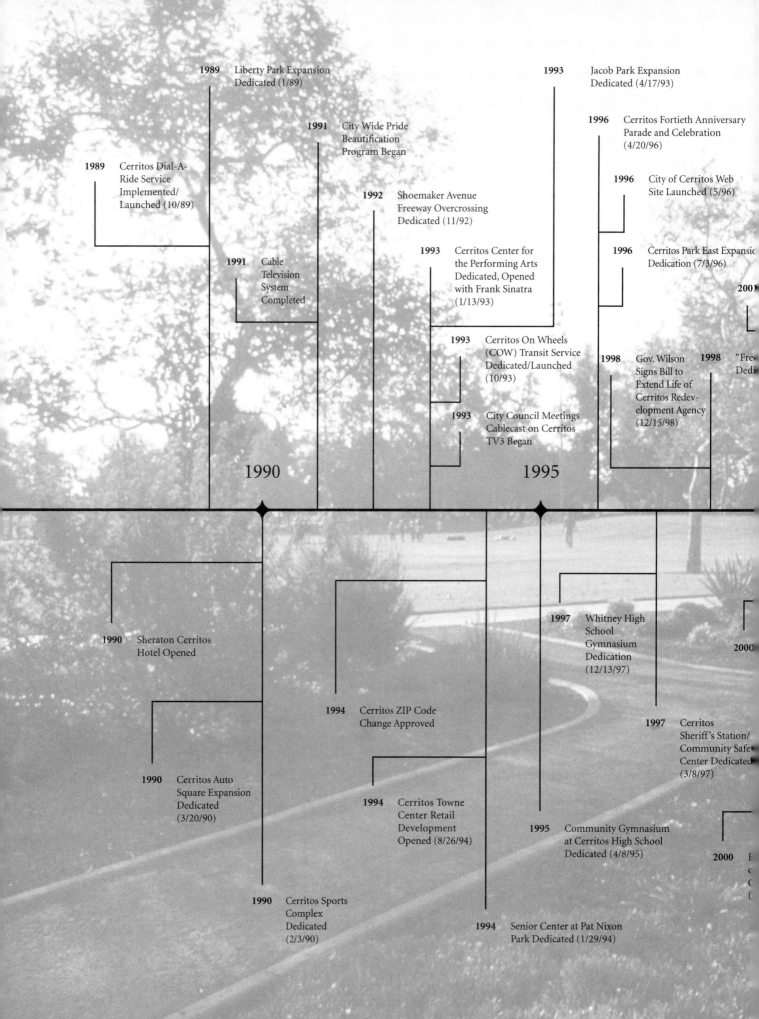

1989 Liberty Park Expansion Dedicated (1/89)

1989 Cerritos Dial-A-Ride Service Implemented/Launched (10/89)

1991 City Wide Pride Beautification Program Began

1991 Cable Television System Completed

1992 Shoemaker Avenue Freeway Overcrossing Dedicated (11/92)

1993 Cerritos Center for the Performing Arts Dedicated, Opened with Frank Sinatra (1/13/93)

1993 Cerritos On Wheels (COW) Transit Service Dedicated/Launched (10/93)

1993 City Council Meetings Cablecast on Cerritos TV3 Began

1993 Jacob Park Expansion Dedicated (4/17/93)

1996 Cerritos Fortieth Anniversary Parade and Celebration (4/20/96)

1996 City of Cerritos Web Site Launched (5/96)

1996 Cerritos Park East Expansion Dedication (7/3/96)

200

1998 Gov. Wilson Signs Bill to Extend Life of Cerritos Redevelopment Agency (12/15/98)

1998 "Fre Ded

1990

1995

1990 Sheraton Cerritos Hotel Opened

1990 Cerritos Auto Square Expansion Dedicated (3/20/90)

1990 Cerritos Sports Complex Dedicated (2/3/90)

1994 Cerritos ZIP Code Change Approved

1994 Cerritos Towne Center Retail Development Opened (8/26/94)

1994 Senior Center at Pat Nixon Park Dedicated (1/29/94)

1997 Whitney High School Gymnasium Dedication (12/13/97)

1997 Cerritos Sheriff's Station/ Community Safe Center Dedicated (3/8/97)

1995 Community Gymnasium at Cerritos High School Dedicated (4/8/95)

2000

2000